Human–Computer Interaction Series

Editor-in-Chief
Desney Tan
Jean Vanderdonckt

More information about this series at http://www.springer.com/series/6033

Katia Vega • Hugo Fuks

Beauty Technology

Designing Seamless Interfaces
for Wearable Computing

 Springer

Katia Vega
Department of Informatics
Pontifical Catholic University
of Rio de Janeiro
Rio de Janeiro, Brazil

Hugo Fuks
Department of Informatics
Pontifical Catholic University
of Rio de Janeiro
Rio de Janeiro, Brazil

ISSN 1571-5035
Human–Computer Interaction Series
ISBN 978-3-319-79220-0   ISBN 978-3-319-15762-7   (eBook)
DOI 10.1007/978-3-319-15762-7

Printed on acid-free paper

This Springer imprint is published by Springer Nature
The registered company is Springer International Publishing AG Switzerland

Preface

This book grew out of our desire to present a compilation of the different Beauty Technologies we have been prototyping since 2012. It presents an exploration of the interaction between the body and technology. Consequently, the prototypes were created in a multidisciplinary fashion: computing, chemistry, body structure, human behavior, electronics, and design were the basis for creating Beauty Technologies.

When we started this project, our aim was to design seamless interfaces using wearables. At that time, most of the wearables we could find in the marketplace were very distinguishable and limited to clothes and accessories, such as a wristband and glasses. Thus, we started to look for the possibilities of having technologies on our body surface. Women from all around the world brought the inspiration for creating Beauty Technology: a Hong Konger putting her fake eyelashes while the bus is in movement, a Japanese girl wearing very long and decorated nails with Swarovski crystals, and an English girl donning the look of longer and fuller hair by using hair extensions. All of them invited us to think about different aspects of the cosmetics industry, where the functionality of cosmetics did not change over the years, i.e., a red lipstick continues to be used for highlighting and coloring the lips (how could we add a new functionality to cosmetics to make them interactive?) and the daily time consumed in cosmetics application at home and beauty parlors (how could we embed electronics into cosmetics, so they could be applied together as cosmetics?).

This book organizes its chapters presenting Beauty Technologies that were developed for each part of the regenerative body surface: skin, fingernails, and hair.

The reader will realize by reading this book that we did not create new gesture interactions: a wink, facial movements, finger movements, and a hair stroke are some of the behaviors that human beings use consciously and unconsciously. In order to conceal interaction with our devices, human behaviors were used in order to create an interactive platform. In this way, a wink made a drone fly, a smile turned on lights, finger movements paid the bus ride, and a hair stroke started the recording of a conversation in a smartphone.

During our prototyping, we have tested a variety of materials and different techniques were used such as the one described in the creation of the Conductive

Makeup. We started using aluminum foils, moving on to the application of conductive ink directly to the skin and eyelashes, and finally rendering them "natural" by chemically metalizing fake eyelashes. We provide the reader with the necessary information to recreate each Beauty Technology presented in this book.

We understand that Beauty Technology is a new subfield in Wearable Computing. Our wish is that researchers will adopt the techniques and lessons learned from this book into their own projects, creating a new batch of interactive cosmetics, new beauty technologies.

Rio de Janeiro, Brazil   Katia Vega
                                                                            Hugo Fuks

Acknowledgments

We are tremendously grateful to the many people who collaborated in the development of Beauty Technology and this book.

We are thankful to the following collaborators in Beauty Technology's prototypes: *Superhero*, EQA (chemical lab) and Jonathan James (costume designer); *Arcana*, Larca Meicap (character conception and makeup) and Maribel Tafur (video); *Blinklifier*, Tricia Flanagan (headdress artist), EQA (chemical lab), Dicky Ma (photo), and Gutekunst/Frey (video); *AquaDJs*, Maribel Tafur (DJ and video), Congo Sanchez, Karla Lara, and Kirin Rider; *Sentido Aware*, Elen Nas (performer) and Camaleão Produtora (video); *Betility*, Constanza Piekarz (belt designer); *Winkymote*, Abel Arrieta (electronic assistant), Felipe Esteves (evaluation), and Natalia Bruno (product designer); and *Kinisi*, Abel Arrieta (electronic assistant), Larca Meicap (character concept and makeup), Juan Carlos Yanaura (direction and edition), Gabriella Chávez (model), Maribel Tafur (music), Aluzcine (production), Marcio Cunha (IoT expert), Rejane Matos and Alan Livio (actors), Maribel Tafur (music), and Tales Cosmo (video).

Felipe Esteves deserves our thanks for being the first person that said that he would use Beauty Technology, inspiring us to create the FX e-makeup for people with disabilities. We thank Hugo Rojas (EQA lab) and Prof. Ricardo Aucélio (PUC-Rio) for sharing their knowledge in chemistry by opening their lab doors for the development of the Conductive Eyelashes and Hairware.

Thank you Prof. Clarisse Sieckenius de Souza (PUC-Rio) for encouraging us to publish this book after Katia's thesis defense. She put us in contact with Beverley Ford (Springer), whom we would also like to thank for leading this project and together with Jorge Nakahara, provided us with a great editorial guidance while preparing this volume.

We are also grateful to the CNPq and CAPES Brazilian agencies for providing the funding that allowed us to do this research. Finally, we would like to thank the Department of Informatics of the Pontifical Catholic University of Rio de Janeiro (PUC-Rio) where the work was done.

Contents

1	**Introduction**	1
	Wearable Computing	1
	New Materials	1
	Wearables Revolution	2
	The Body as a Design Platform	2
	Cosmetics	3
	A Very Brief History of Cosmetics	3
	Cyborg Fashion	4
	On the Content and Structure of This Book	6
2	**Beauty Technology Definition**	9
	Related Technologies	9
	Beauty Technology: Context of Application	12
	From Traditional to Interactive Cosmetics	13
3	**Hair Interfaces**	17
	Conductive Eyelashes	17
	Interfaces for Sensing Blinking	17
	Blinking Interaction	18
	Conductive Makeup Design	20
	Conductive Makeup Prototypes: Electronic Divas	20
	Lessons Learned	24
	Hairware	27
	Hair Interfaces	27
	Designing Hairware	28
	Hairware as an Output Device	30
	Hairware as an Input Device	31
	Lessons Learned	40

4 Skin Interfaces.. 43
   Interfaces on the Skin... 43
   FX e-makeup.. 43
      Interfaces for Sensing Facial Actions 44
      FX e-makeup Design 45
      FX e-makeup Prototypes.. 46
      Lessons Learned... 52

5 Nail Interfaces 57
   Interfaces on Fingertips.. 57
   Beauty Tech Nails with RFIDs 58
      RFID Based Interaction 59
   Tech Nails Design 60
   Interactive Possibilities and Prototypes 60
      Non-contact Interaction 61
      Interactions from Tech Nails to Wearables.............................. 61
      Unusual Interactions 63
   Lessons Learned.. 68

6 Final Consideration 69
   Beauty Technologies by Sectors 71
      Glamor Sector... 71
      Communication Sector.. 73
      Lifestyle Computing Sector 73
      Sport and Fitness.. 73
      Wellness 74
      Medical 74
      Security and Safety 74

Annex 1   Awards 77

Annex 2   Publications 79

Annex 3   Exhibitions and Demos... 81

Annex 4   Media Coverage 83

References.. 101

Index.. 109

Chapter 1
Introduction

Wearable Computing

The idea behind augmenting human capabilities through Wearable Technologies has a long history starting with eyeglasses and pocket watches, created to augment sight and to track time [1]. Robert Hooke [2] proposed the idea of adding "artificial organs" to our natural ones in order to improve our hearing, smelling, tasting, and touching. Today, Wearable Computing is looking for opportunities to integrate computational and sensory devices to the body in a way that inextricably intertwine human and computer [3].

New Materials

Developments in novel materials are improving the ease of embedding technologies into fabrics as well as the use of implantable devices and biosensors [4]. Nanotechnology, biotechnology, information technology and cognitive technology are converging—making it possible to foresee wearables with their own power generation, flexible displays and electric-responsive materials [5].

The evolution of computation from desktop to on body led to the creation of smart clothing, also called e-textiles, that intertwine electronic components into yarn [6–8]. Lilypad Arduino was one of the first kits on the market that included sensors and actuators for connecting to a microcontroller by using conductive thread and conductive fabrics in order to camouflage a circuit in clothing [9]. Batteries and super capacitors are also been studied as a way to be integrated with e-textiles. Such are the cases of Solar Fibers [10] that convert sunlight into electrical energy by using flexible photovoltaic fiber and flexible storage devices

© Springer International Publishing Switzerland 2016
K. Vega, H. Fuks, *Beauty Technology*, Human–Computer Interaction Series,
DOI 10.1007/978-3-319-15762-7_1

[11] that use nanocomposite paper for creating energy storage devices. Moreover, our own body can be used as a source of energy: from using piezoelectric for capturing energy while walking [12] to the use of jewelry on the body surface that converts involuntary movements into energy [13].

Unlike other tangibles where electronics are covered by a plastic box, wearable devices, especially the ones that are in/on the skin, must deal with human body characteristics such as skin temperature and perspiration, and with human movements such as flexing joints and bending the skin. For this reason, researchers are using nanomaterials for creating epidermal electronics that act as removable tattoos for health monitoring [14], and electronic skins that, in a similar way, are used as bandages [15].

Wearables Revolution

The fact that big software companies such as Google, Motorola, Apple and Microsoft are creating wearables, and also the fashion industry icons like Nike and Adidas are making significant investments in this area is an indicator that wearables will become mainstream in the forthcoming years [4]. Google Glass [16] is one of the clearest examples of wearables that have garnered great attention in recent years. These glasses embed a display coupled with a location awareness sensor, illustrating the potential of wearable technologies to tap into apps enabling users to access information. Start-ups are also investing in wearables technologies. For example, Pebble [17] created a wristwatch designed to interact with an iPhone and in a short period of time it has broken records on the Kickstarter crowdfunding platform.

Besides this revolution in wearable gadgets at the marketplace, wearable computing has become an interdisciplinary field. Wearables will be exclusive neither for fashion designers, nor for electronic engineers. It is expected that professionals with different skills will get together and share their knowledge to create novel technologies. This opens the Do-It-Yourself (DIY) gateway for hobbyists, enthusiasts and researchers in different fields to design their own wearables. Adafruit, Seeed Studio and Sparkfun are some of the stores where makers purchase their components, accompanied by detailed tutorials, especially tailored for wearable computing [18–20]. Moreover, hardware companies such as Intel are offering new microcontrollers such the Intel Edison and Curie [21] for the makers' community with a view to wearable computing.

The Body as a Design Platform

Wearables are already causing a rethinking of the boundaries of the body. Lucy McRae [22] envisions future possibilities of merging technology and the human body. Through artistic showcases, she redefines the body by mimicking its musculature,

Fig. 1.1 LED eyelashes [24]. Courtesy of Soomi Park

thus, changing the perception of our own body to create futuristic human shapes. Along these lines, LED eyelashes [23] expose the desire of many Asian women to show more of their eyes by lighting the eyelashes that follow pupil and head movements (Fig. 1.1).

Cosmetics

A Very Brief History of Cosmetics

Cosmetics are an important part of human personal history. Their use varies from cultural and religious aspects such as displaying national pride, to camouflage when hunting or fighting, but mostly for augmenting and hiding our physical features in order to enhance appearance.

However, why do cosmetics have always being important to human beings?

Africans were, probably, the one that had the earliest cosmetics in human history. Kohl and henna are raw materials that are originally from Africa and had being found in cosmetics from different civilizations [25]. In the Blombos Cave in South Africa, they found a 100,000 years old paint factory that were used for canvas. These paints could also be used to paint patterns on the skin [26].

Ancient Egyptians used cosmetics not only for its aesthetically and healthy purpose, but also for a spiritual use [27]. Oils and creams protected their skin from sun and dry weather and were also used for religious rituals and embalming the death [28]. They are well known for their black eyeliner makeup. Surprisingly, the kohl black line was not used for appealing the Egyptian looks, it was used to prevent ocular infection [29].

When cosmetics arrived to Greece and Italy, they won an aesthetic connotation. However, in both civilizations women were criticized for the excessive and hazardous use of cosmetics [30]. Greek women were credited to be the first to use white lead facial cream in order to have pale faces [31]. Roman cosmetics inventions include the use of walnut extracts to darken hair and germander to make it red [30]. Chinese colored and maintained long their fingernails for differentiating between social classes [32]. More radically, Chinese non aristocratic women wearing them in public were executed and in Japan, women from high hierarchy were not allowed to appear in public without their cosmetic treatments [33].

In the Middle Ages, because of the Crusades, perfumes were popularized in Europe. Queen Elizabeth I changed the beauty standards by innovating in cosmetic fashion, inspiring many women to use red cheeks, pale skin and having their hair and skinny eyebrows dyed reddish. Moreover, red lines simulating veins were drawn in a sign of age [30]. In the Renaissance, only Europe aristocracy used cosmetics and the first cosmetic manufactures were created in France and Italy [28].

Nowadays, it seems that more than ever we are concerned of the effect of cosmetics. People browse gossip magazines to see how bad celebrities look without wearing makeup and whatever they wear, leads the cosmetics fashion. Customers are more demanding on the toxicity of the products and companies are increasingly improving their testing techniques such as the use of 3D printing skins [34] and avoiding animals for evaluating their products [35]. Cosmetics manufacturing are regulated by each country agency such as Food and Drugs Administration (FDA) in United States [36]. Women spend hours in different treatments at the saloon and plastic surgeries are on high demand in order to keep a youth appearance.

An estimated 85 % of women support a $382 billion global beauty business market dominated by multinational corporations [37]. It is estimated that the U.S. cosmetic industry amounted to about $62 billion in 2016 [38]. Data from a 2014 survey [39] state that adult women spent 55 min in front of the mirror everyday using in average five items in their daily routines.

Cyborg Fashion

The word cyborg is a mash up of the phrase "cybernetic organism" and was coined more than 50 years ago in an academic article on the possible future needs for humans surviving in extra-terrestrial environments [40]. It described the advantages of a self-regulatory human-machine system, adjusted to the space environment, in which "robot-like problems are taken care of automatically and unconsciously, leaving man free to explore, to create, to think, and to feel" [40]. Despite some critical reviews like the one in Popular Science [41] that exposed the image of the "tomorrow's man" with technological gadgets around his body, the term cyborg is considered by most futuristic predictions to present how human's capability will be augmented through technology. For example, The Singularity, which is a theoretical point in time where technology will have progressed to the point that humans will augment their bodies and increase their life spans through enhancements, predicts that humans will become cyborgs by 2045 [42].

Literature, art and film always devise possible futures that new technologies might bring. Their predictions and projections not only shape ways of imagining the future of humanity, but have also prepared us to adapt to and gradually accept the ideas of a technologically mediated existence [43]. Most notably Martin Caidin's novel entitled Cyborg (1972) was adapted as TV's Six Million Dollar Man, in which a former astronaut with bionic implants works for a fictional government office [44]. By the 1980s, when the idea of a direct human interface with computers was taken seriously, "cyberpunk" readers were littered with imaginary cyborgs. Prosthetic devices to enhance and extend the range and function of human vision are probably the most common of cyborg systems in contemporary science fiction. Locutus had the Borg's cybernetic devices implanted throughout his body in Star Trek: The Next Generation. Terminator, Robocop and Darth Vader are fictional cyborgs wearing a metal endoskeleton, on-board computer assisted memory and cybernetic limbs. Science-fiction movies and the depiction of human-computer interaction and communication have been closely intertwined by necessity. Nowadays, there are cyborgs inhabiting our cities helped by the Cyborg Foundation [45]. Figure 1.2 presents Neil Harbisson, the first official cyborg carrying a wearable device implanted on his skull that transmits sounds via bone conduction. On the other hand, other gadgets propose the use of clothing and accessories for hidden technology. This is the case of Project Jacquard [46], the recent partnership between Google and Levis that produces jeans with tiny circuits connected through conductive yarns to capture touch interactions. Ringly [47] is another example that makes the technology seamless having a ring shape that receives notifications from a smartphone. Ralph Lauren's Polo Tech shirt [48] is also a seamless fashionable technology that reminds a classic sport t-shirt incorporating sensors hidden into the fabric for measuring the user fitness performance.

Due to the proximity with the body, the term cyborg is commonly associated with wearables, and science fiction has foretold the merging of man and machine for many years, but it is usually presented as a human with electronics emerging from his body. For instance, one of the arguments against the early adoption of wearables is their cyborg look. If we take Mark Weiser's vision [50] seriously, we will no doubt recognize that current wearables are nevertheless very distinguishable. In this project, we propose cyborg interfaces without having their stereotypical visual aesthetics.

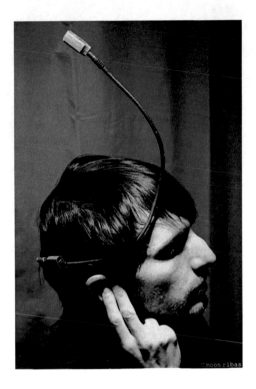

On the Content and Structure of This Book

This book is targeted at HCI researchers, makers, makeup artists, musicians, researchers on assistive technologies, wearable computing developers and to those who are interested in the design of wearables for the body surface, the search for novel materials that transform the body in an interface and the intersection between the body and technology.

Due to the big wave of wearable gadgets at the marketplace and the demand for innovative design, seamless interfaces became a winner option for designing wearables where the electronics are not noticeable. We differentiate ours from other wearables because our aim is to locate them directly on the body surface, instead of on clothing and accessories, and to conceal them.

This book is divided into six chapters. Next chapter describes Beauty Technology and its application context. Chapters 3, 4 and 5 present Beauty Technologies applied to hair, skin and nails, respectively. Figure 1.3 shows this organization. The final chapter presents the conclusions and future work on Beauty Technology.

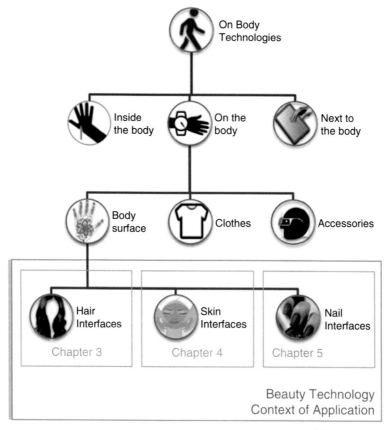

Fig. 1.3 Beauty technology book organization

Chapter 2
Beauty Technology Definition

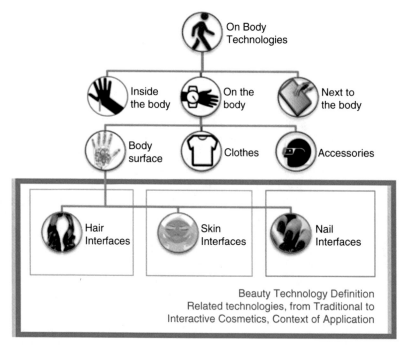

Fig. 2.1 Chapter 2: Beauty technology definition

© Springer International Publishing Switzerland 2016
K. Vega, H. Fuks, *Beauty Technology*, Human–Computer Interaction Series,
DOI 10.1007/978-3-319-15762-7_2

Related Technologies

Aristotle (384–322 BC) is credited with the original classification of the five senses: sight, smell, taste, touch, and hearing [51] that link us to the external world. As far back as the 1760s, the philosopher Immanuel Kant proposed that our knowledge of the outside world depends on our modes of perception [52]. Nevertheless, even if we are immediately aware of changes in our environment, our attention to specific targets is limited by the brain's ability to process these stimuli sequentially. Our reflexes react to all stimuli arriving simultaneously to our sensory environment. However, there are lapses in awareness of seemingly obvious stimuli to temporary losses of attention and lapses that we are not aware of in the form of reflexes.

Bio data is not expected to be used to predict all future behaviors but it is useful in personnel selection because it can give an indication of probable future behaviors based on an individual's prior learning history [53]. Humanistic Intelligence proposed by Mann [3] describes a framework where the natural capabilities of the human body and mind interact in synergy with one another and wearables become an integral part of the feedback loop.

Humans use a wide variety of muscles for creating gestures. They range from simple actions of using the hand to point at objects to the more complex actions that express feelings and communicate with others. Muscle movements are a clear representation of a user's intent [54]. When we initiate a voluntary movement, the brain sends an electrochemical signal that traverses our nervous system through the spinal cord and eventually arrives at the motor neurons. They stimulate our muscles causing movement or force [55]. Several sensors are used on wearables to capture movements and other bio data. They are placed in different parts of the body depending on the measurement to get: respiration sensor, pulse sensor, pressure sensor, electroencephalogram (EEG), electromyogram (EMG), electrooculogram (EOG), electrocardiogram (ECG), visual sensor, sink mode, accelerator and gyroscope [56]. For example, EMG detects muscular movements by gel-based sensors firmly held in place with adhesives [54, 57] and accelerators on different part of the body detect body posture and movements [58].

Computational vision also offers a possibility for hands-free interfaces to sense movements and gestures [59]. However, it presents some issues like occlusion and lighting that limit the opportunities for its use [60]. By using wearables and computer vision techniques for tracking macro movements, it is possible to interpret pose and motion. Most approaches use machine learning algorithms and classifiers based on graphical models for macro movement recognition. For example, a skeleton model is often used in Kinect applications. It currently is a tree-graph consisting of 20 nodes corresponding to certain key joints in the human body [61]. Usually a set of parameters such as joint locations, velocities and accelerations are used to localize and track movements. Another example is SixthSense [62] that is a wearable that includes a camera and a projector that recognizes different objects in the

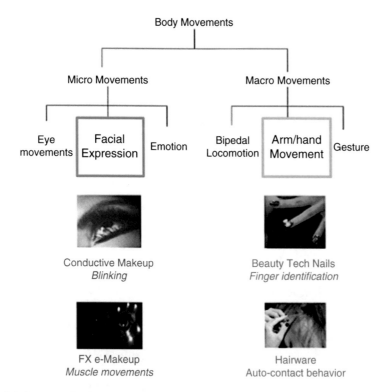

Fig. 2.2 Beauty technologies on the taxonomy of body movements, adapted from [64]

environment and gestures done by the user's fingers and hands. Armura [63] is an on body computer interface that tracks the location of the arms and hands, as well as recognizes their gestural state and provides graphical feedback onto the body.

Human Computer Interaction studies movements as explicit and implicit inputs. Abawajy proposed a taxonomy of Body Movements with respect to HCI [64]. It classifies movements into Micro Movements (eye movement, facial expression and emotion) and Macro Movements (bipedal locomotion, arm/hand movement and gestures). This project uses a muscle-based strategy for sensing movements as inputs. Figure 2.2 shows current Beauty Technologies and their relation to this taxonomy. New Beauty Technologies may be created around other body movements and extended by other sensors and actuators.

Nonverbal human interaction, facial expressions and body gestures communicate emotional content [65]. Thus, facial expression recognition has attracted the interest of the artificial intelligence and computer vision communities mainly for identification of human emotions [66] and security. Beauty Technologies such as Conductive Makeup and FX e-makeup, interpret facial expression Micro movements like blinking and facial movements.

Fine motor system coordinates fine muscle movements in body parts such as the fingers, usually in coordination with the eyes. In relation to motor skills of hands and fingers, the term dexterity is commonly used. The independent control of finger movements is a key feature of the dexterous use of the hand. A superior independence of finger movements in humans over non-human primates indicates the development of this motor function in parallel with the evolution of an ability to manipulate various tools [67]. Tech Nails and Hairware are other examples of Beauty Technologies that interpret arm/hand Macro movements such as finger movement and hair touch, respectively.

Beauty Technology: Context of Application

The human body became an important topic in the field of HCI due to the proximity of wearables to the body and the aim of processing user's data in everyday objects. The different body features such as form, texture and temperature must be considered in the creation of wearables. On body technologies normally take the form of electronic portable devices. Figure 2.3 shows our classification of on body technologies, focusing on the context of Beauty Technology. In this way, technology can be on the body such as wearables, technology can be inside the body such as implants and carried next to the body such as mobile computers. The main difference between mobile computers and wearables is that the former often requires your full attention and the use of both hands to be operated [68]. Instead of embedding electronics into clothing, that is a familiar object for humans, mobile computers are electronics created for a specific purpose and with a specific shape. Wearables can be placed not just for clothes and accessories, but also on the top of the body's surface.

Skin and its appendages (i.e. hair and nails) are regenerative organs that play a crucial role in human beings as: a protective barrier, a sensory input from the environment, a heat and moisture regulator and a part of the immune system [69]. Moreover, they have being manipulated using tattoos and beauty products since the earliest days of the human race [32].

Figure 2.4 shows Pearson's vision [5] defining multiple layers of technology into/onto the skin and communication possibilities through these layers. The Wearable layer sits on the body like a watch. The Membrane layer sits just on the skins surface and not into it. On this layer, technologies are placed onto the skin surface and can be easily removed. Beauty Technologies operate on this layer. The Printed layer places fully removable devices on the epidermis that are only worn on a temporary basis, but are interacting with the layers below. The Mid-term layer is also in the skin but it gradually wears away over time with the skin dead cells. The Permanent layer permanently prints technology into the lowest layer of the epidermis. This project lists technologies that are not necessarily available; it offers researchers the inspiration to create them.

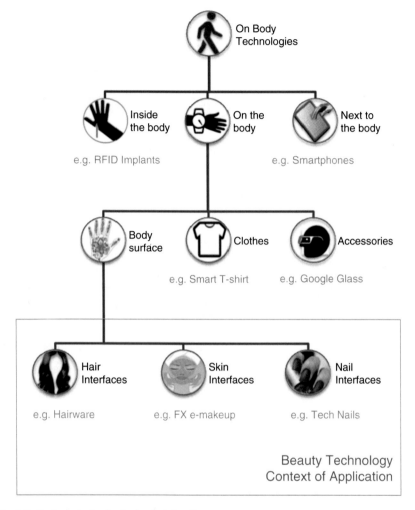

Fig. 2.3 On body technologies by their locality

From Traditional to Interactive Cosmetics

Digital technology is omnipresent in our daily life. Smartphones, e-commerce and social networking influence the way people interact with others everywhere in the world. It is common to buy cosmetics on the Internet and learn how to apply them by watching online tutorials. Smartphone apps help us to match our skin and outfit. For example, Makeup Genius from L'Oreal is an app that works like a mirror making it possible to test cosmetics [71]. Moreover, wearables are being created for supporting beauty—Sunfriend monitors our daily ultraviolet radiation intake to alert when it is the best time to reapply

Fig. 2.4 Multilayer classification of devices on the skin [70]. Courtesy of Ian Pearson

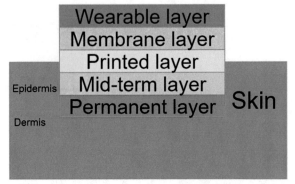

Skin-based electronics can link blood chemistry and nerve signals to external computers and systems

more sunscreen [72]. In addition, DIY machines such as 3D printers make it possible to create personalized cosmetics. Mink is a 3D printer that creates eye shadows in any color [73]. 3D Bioprinting aims to print living cells in order to create a human skin for testing L'Oreal products without using animals. Wanderers make use of living materials for 3D printing wearables with bacteria for augmenting the environment [74].

Each country has its own laws and regulation institutes that norm the safety and effectiveness of cosmetics. The U.S. Food and Drug Administration defines cosmetics as articles intended to be rubbed, poured, sprinkled, or sprayed on, introduced into, or otherwise applied to the human body or any part thereof for cleansing, beautifying, promoting attractiveness, or altering the appearance [36]. For centuries, these have been the cosmetics main features. Moisturizers have been used for hydrating the skin, lipstick to color our lips, shampoo for cleaning our hair. Several technologies improved their manufacture process but, at the end of the day, the functionality of cosmetics did not change over time. Beauty Technology add new features to cosmetics by using electronic components. Table 2.1 presents some examples of Beauty Technologies that extend the uses of cosmetics. In this way, cosmetics will remain being used for cleansing, beautifying, promoting attractiveness and altering appearance, and in addition, being part of the Internet of Things.

Table 2.1 From traditional cosmetics to interactive cosmetics

	Non interactive cosmetics	Interactive cosmetics: Beauty technology
Beautifying	**Moisturizer** Hydrates the skin	**e-Moisturizer** Hydrates skin depending on weather and skin properties
Promoting attractiveness	**Eye makeup** Highlights eyes	**Conductive makeup** [75] Highlights eyes and turns on devices by blinking
	Nail polish Colors fingernails	**Tech nails** [76] Colorizes fingernails and opens the door, pays the metro, interactive performances with RFID nails **Lumi deco nails** [77] Colorizes fingernails and turn on LEDs in fingernails when receiving a call
Altering the appearance	**Special effects makeup** Skin body parts with different effects	**FX e-makeup** [78] Skin body parts that embeds sensors in latex for sensing muscle movements: a wink, a smile, an eyebrow raise
	Tattoos Permanent designs in the skin	**iSkin** [79] Designs on the skin with flexible biomaterial that detects touch input **AERIALS** [80] Designs on the skin with RFIDs tattooed
Cleansing	**Deodorant** Imparts fragrance to the user	**e-Deodorant** Imparts fragrance to the user and stamps an RFID for user recognition

Chapter 3
Hair Interfaces

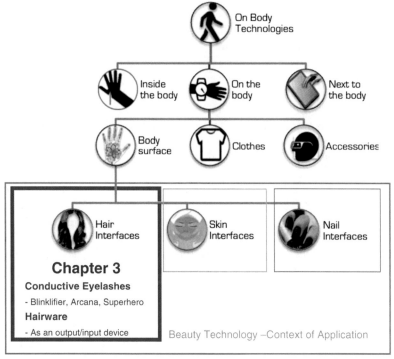

Fig. 3.1 Hair Interfaces

© Springer International Publishing Switzerland 2016
K. Vega, H. Fuks, *Beauty Technology*, Human–Computer Interaction Series,
DOI 10.1007/978-3-319-15762-7_3

Conductive Eyelashes

As the eyes are a rich source of information for gathering context in our everyday lives, HCI researchers have investigated the potential of eye movement as a form of input. Six extrinsic muscles allow for vertical, horizontal and rotational movements of the eyeball. BlinkBot [81] is a hands free input interface that control and command a robot. It uses gaze and blinking as input instructions to direct a robot to move an object from one location to another.

Interfaces for Sensing Blinking

The nature of the human visual system is such that high resolution is restricted to a small area, requiring the gaze to shift to each area of interest, indicating changes in visual attention and reflecting the cognitive states of the individual [82]. These eye movements have been studied in an effort to derive finer indicators of cognitive activity such as reading, searching and exploring. The human eye has also been used as a hands free input device. For example, a user blinks and makes left/right winking combinations to completely control a system by using Blinkbot [81].

Blinking could be sensed by both vision and non-vision computational techniques. Non-vision techniques include electrooculography (EOG) and high frequency transceivers. When humans initiate a voluntary action, the brain sends an electrochemical signal that traverses our nervous system through the spinal cord and eventually reaches the motor neurons. They stimulate specific muscles causing movement or force [55]. Being used for detecting muscular movements, an EOG signal is based on electrical measurement of the potential difference between the cornea and the retina. The cornea-retinal potential creates an electrical field in the front of the head. Electrodes placed near the eyes detect changes in electricity. In this technique, users must wear gel-based sensors attached to their muscles with strong adhesives [54, 57] or goggles coupled with electrodes integrated into the frame that records EOG signals [83].

Computational vision methods for blinking detection are divided into two groups namely, active and passive. The active blinking detection technique requires special illumination to capture the retro-reflective property of the eye. The camera identifies a reflected beam on the pupil when the light source focusses on the focal axis of the camera. On the other hand, passive blinking detection methods do not use any additional light sources. Blinking is detected from the sequence of images within the visible spectrum in natural illumination conditions. They use different approaches for this purpose, such as template matching [84], skin color models [85], projection [86] and directional Circle Hough Transform [87].

Blinking Interaction

Certain external factors or conditions affect the natural process of blinking [88]. Blinking is classified as endogenous, reflexive or voluntary [89]. The endogenous one is identified as a cortically controlled response event, distinguishable from other blinks by the absence of an identifiable eliciting stimulus. It is the body's way of spreading tears and moisture across the eye. The blinking reflex is a protective response that occurs as stimuli to avoid potential injuries to the organism. Thus, it responses when something invades the eye, like air puffs or dust, and it is part of our fright reaction to loud noises. The voluntary blinking takes place in response to an identifiable stimulus, either self-initiated or at the request of a researcher [88]. Microsleep, being regarded as a non-blink closure, is observed in sleep-deprived or otherwise fatigued individuals.

Blinking takes place approximately 10–15 times per minute. The normal duration of blinking is in between 150 and 250 ms and the longest closure period during blinking is estimated to be 270–300 ms [90]. To use blinking as a means of triggering, we defined a voluntary blinking closure duration that falls between a pre-set minimal and maximal duration. Based on this data, we estimate that the range in Beauty Technology prototypes is between 0.5 and 2 s. Therefore, any eye closure that satisfies this criterion is regarded as a blinking trigger. Voluntary long blinking triggers smart objects, while involuntary short blinking are simply ignored. In addition, a combination of blinking can be identified as one or a sequence of instructions for interaction.

Figure 3.2 shows a drawing of a user wearing the Conductive Makeup: Conductive Eyelashes, Conductive Makeup and a circuit. Conductive Makeup prototypes make use of blinking as input for triggering different devices such as appliances, smartphones and computers. The eyeliner must be precisely applied on the eyelids

Fig. 3.2 Conductive makeup blinking interface

in a way that the upper and lower eyelashes only make contact when the eye is closed. The eyeliner connects the conductive fake eyelashes to the circuit. The conductive eyelashes work like a switch that is off when the eye is open and on when the eye is totally closed. A circuit hidden into a wig or headband processes these digital signs. In addition, it could interact with other devices that are connected to a wireless network. For example, when the user closes her left eye, a digital sign is sent via a radio module. The circuit that includes the radio module and the connections to the eyelashes is hidden inside the headband. Other radio modules can be used to interact with a computer, a smart object or another wearable.

Conductive Makeup Design

In order to avoid using any electronic component on the wearer's face, skin conductive material is applied as black eyeliner to connect conductive fake eyelashes to a headband. This eyeliner is a conductive tape that starts with the shape of an upper or lower eyelid and terminates as a slight line. A black paint covers the silver color giving it a black eyeliner look. These eyeliners are placed in parallel using human skin glue that sticks the eyeliner in position and at the same time, isolates the conductivity from the skin.

The eyelashes are chemically metalized in order to mimic the natural black color of the eyelashes. The chemical process is carried out in two phases namely, activation and electrolysis. During the first phase, the fake eyelashes, being plastic nonconducting surfaces, require some kind of activation to enable them to be used in an electrochemical process. The first activation is achieved using hydrogen and tin chloride. After that, a silver nitrate solution is added for the second activation, setting up the eyelashes as catalysts of electron transfer reactions and ready for metalizing. The electrolysis phase deposits a layer of nickel on the eyelashes to plate them. It uses copper for making the eyelashes electrically conductive and black nickel for the natural black effect of the eyelashes. Figure 3.3 shows one of the phases of the electrochemical process. Table 3.1 shows the formulations and time needed for creating Black Metalized Fake Eyelashes.

Conductive Makeup Prototypes: Electronic Divas

Technologies for sensing information in personal spaces like blinking, pulse rates and respiration monitoring have advanced in recent years [56]. In parallel technologies for communicating with smart spaces, smart objects, wearables, virtual worlds and social networks have also experienced many improvements in recent years. These technologies enhance human capabilities and we foresee the use of wearables becoming a key component for interaction. With this evolutionary technology and our aim of hiding embedded electronics in everyday life objects, we put forward Electronic Divas: individuals empowered with Beauty Technology based on Conductive Makeup. When they blink, objects levitate and sound tracks change.

Fig. 3.3 Metalizing black fake eyelashes

By wearing Beauty Technologies, they amplify their capabilities, sense the world and highlight their personalities.

Arcana, Blinklifier and Superhero incarnated our Electronic Divas in several performances and art exhibitions. Specific tasks were associated with winking the left and the right eyes, and closing both eyes. These gestures trigger actuators connected to circuits and communicate with other wireless external devices.

The Blinklifier project began as a collaboration of three artists: a Japanese painter, a Chinese fashion designer and an Australian artist where a Japanese-inspired painting was turned into a fashionable dress and a matching headdress. By embedding technology into this headdress, a new collaboration between art and technology fostered the creation of Blinklifier. By responding to specific eye movement patterns, it communicates emotions by presenting noticeable, exaggerated visual compositions. It uses 72 LEDs to create blinking patterns on the headdress (Fig. 3.4). Different light patterns show up when the wearer winks with her left, right, opens and closes her eyes. The Blinklifier piece was shown in several exhibitions [91–94]. The video is available at https://youtu.be/rymbYGpr15g.

Arcana is another collaborative project with a makeup artist and an actress. Arcana is a futuristic angel that through blinking changes musical tracks and images creating a different world around her. Her eyes, using the conductive makeup, are connected to a headband that hides a radio module that connects to a second radio

Table 3.1 Black metalized fake eyelashes electrochemical process

	Formulation		Temp (°C)	Time (min)
Activation 1	1	Liter of solution	21	5
	10	Grams of SnCl2		
	40	mL of HCl		
Activation 2	1	Liter of solution	21	5
	2	Grams of $AgNO_3$		
	10	Milliliters of NH_3		
Copper electrolysis	1	Liter of solution	40	10
	14	Grams of $CuSO_4$		
	30	Grams of potassium sodium tartrate		
	10	Grams of NaOH		
	40	Milliliters of formaldehyde		
Copper acid	1	Liter of solution	21	10
	220	Grams of copper sulphate pent hydrate		
	34	Milliliters of sulphuric acid		
	10	Milliliters of cupracid solution		
	0.5	Milliliters cupracid brightener 210 Part A		
	0.5	Milliliters cupracid brightener 210 Part B		
	0.12	Grams sodium chloride		
Black nickel	1	Liter of solution	21	10
	120	Grams of nickel sulphate		
	40	Grams of nickel chloride		

module. This one is connected to a computer that identifies the blinking that falls into the range criteria, activating specific music tracks, and changing the visual images (Fig. 3.5). One performance took place in an auditorium showing the projected images displayed on the actress [95]. Figure 3.6 shows Arcana when she winks her right eye. The video is available at https://youtu.be/s_NwChqf45E.

TEI 2013 Design Challenge [96] challenged students with the task of celebrating TEI creativity with a game or performance. Our winner Superhero project made use of the aforementioned conductive makeup and black fake eyelashes, making it possible for the wearer to levitate objects through blinking. Eyelashes worked like switches connected to a circuit sending signals via a radio module to a nearby Superhero Handbag that housed a radio receiver. Accordingly, animated images were displayed (POW, BAM, ZAP) and infrared commands decoded from a remote controller's protocol in order to make an object fly. Figure 3.7 shows the Superhero levitating an object by winking the right eye and Fig. 3.8 shows the Superhero circuit schema. There is a Music Technology Group video available at https://youtu.be/IeTIE6lMiK0.

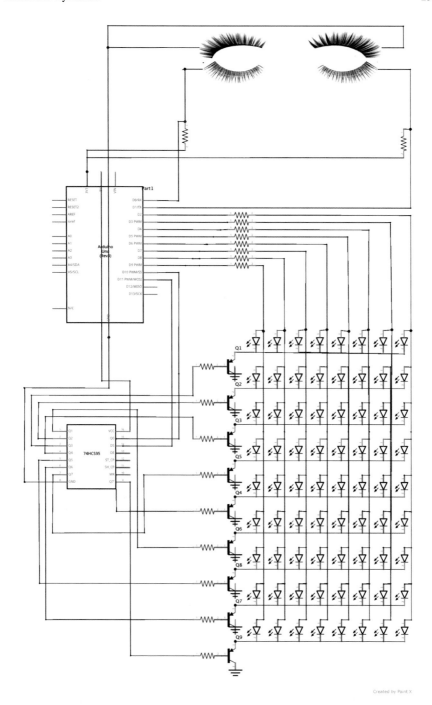

Fig. 3.4 Blinklifier circuit schematics

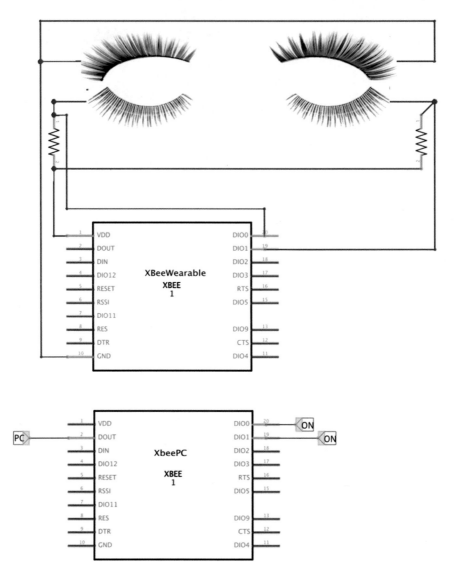

Fig. 3.5 Arcana circuit schematics

Lessons Learned

Cutting aluminum foil into eyelash shapes created the first prototype for the eyelashes. The silver color conflicted with our goal of keeping the natural appearance of black eyelashes. They also lost their shape due to their own weight.

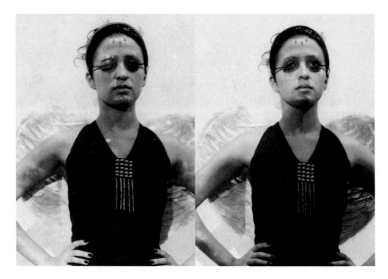

Fig. 3.6 Arcana performance with conductive makeup. Image reproduced with permission from Camila Lopez

Another attempt to make conductive makeup was pursued using conductive ink [97]. This ink was used to draw a line on the eyes and it was applied to the plastic eyelashes as mascara. Bare Conductive states that "though Bare Paint is a material that is safe to have around the body, it is not specifically approved for use on the skin" [97]. Moreover, due to the humidity of the eyes and skin, this ink could be dissipated into the eye. Another issue regarding the use of conductive ink is that it loses conductivity when dried ink split due to skin flexibility and muscle movements.

While continuously sensing voluntary blinking, one issue that interfered with the signal were facial expressions that involved the eye closure like smiling. Future work will include other sensors in different facial muscles for differentiating these movements.

The Electronic Divas wore the same conductive makeup (eyelashes and eyeliner) eight times in testing and performances: Blinklifier (twice), Superhero (five times) and Arcana (once). It required precise application on the skin using special glue. After wearing it for three times, the skin glue isolated some parts of the eyelashes, which then required special cleaning to keep it conductive for the following applications.

The three prototypes ran with a time gap preset to sense voluntary blinking (0.5–2 s). A left and right wink and both eyes closed triggered three different tasks in each prototype. Further work will include blinking combinations designed to produce other output options. For example, winking the left eye for 4 s followed by 2 s of both eyes closed could change a new image in the Superhero prototype.

It is common knowledge that muscles control objects that are part of our daily lives like cars and computers. Makeup is also part of our daily lives and it is used to enhance the appearance of human bodies. Our proposal makes use of Conductive Makeup applied to the face to sense its muscles. We focus on the human agency for controlling the eyes' muscles, specifically voluntary blinking.

Fig. 3.7 Superhero blinks
for levitating objects

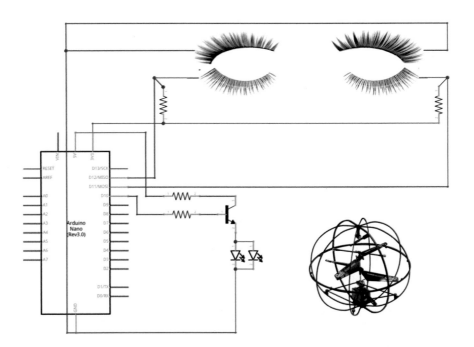

Fig. 3.8 Superhero circuit schematics

Prototypes were developed as proof of concept of the feasibility of Beauty Technology. Blinklifier uses blinking to control LED switching on an artistic head-dress, and in the case of Arcana, for changing music tracks and visual images. Superhero also makes use of Conductive Makeup for levitating an object.

We will explore blinking time duration and combinations for controlling different devices like air conditioning and hospital beds. Other future potential uses of this technology envisage opportunities for empowering individuals with disabilities, hands free interfaces, art performances that expose a gesture, unnoticed gestures as inputs, keeping people awake, and decoding blinking gestures for physical and physiological analysis.

Hairware

Hairware fosters a seamlessly looking approach to wearables. They are artificial hair extensions that are chemically metalized to maintain a natural coloration and when connected to a microcontroller could be used as both, input and output devices [98–100]. This section describes the process used to prototype conductive hair extensions and discusses lessons learned in the development of this Beauty Technology.

Hair Interfaces

Developments in novel materials are improving the ease of embedding technologies into fabrics as well as the use of implantable devices and biosensors [4]. Nanotechnology, biotechnology, information technology and cognitive technology are converging—making it possible to foresee wearables with their own power generation, flexible displays and electric-responsive materials [5]. Even more, the miniaturization and availability of electronic components has made it possible the widespread adoption of wearable computing, moving from the realm of science fiction to the marketplace in areas such as fashion, health, and wellness for the aging and the disabled. Fibrous materials, such as textile and paper, are flexible, foldable, easily cut and attached to flexible substrates. Once they get electrical conductivity and good mechanical endurance against external deformation, they become attractive for flexible and wearable electronics [101]. Conductive fabrics created for wearables are already at the marketplace. Conductive yarn, plated fabric, printing on fabric, and sewing on fabric are some approaches to create e-textiles that are used to embed electronics into textiles [102]. For example, Project Jacquard [46] plans to connect tiny electronic components through conductive yarn in order to create jeans that detects different touches and communicates with an smartphone.

Conductive materials are also being created in this project. Section Conductive Eyelashes above presented Conductive Makeup [75, 103, 104] that is an aesthetic interface for detecting voluntary blinking (Fig. 3.9). The eyelashes were metalized using a chemical process. Thus, showing the possibility of metalizing this kind of material, obtaining in this way a natural coloration without mixing them, regardless the thinness of each eyelash.

Fig. 3.9 Conductive makeup. (**a**) Conductive eyelashes and eyeliner in natural coloration. (**b**) Superhero project that levitates a drone by blinking

Mainly women for dressing up used wigs and accessories. Currently there are some researchers using them as wearables devices. SmartWig [105] is a wearable gadget that uses the base of a wig for hiding electronics that communicates wirelessly with other external devices. SmartWig suggests applications that could fulfill a number of functions, from acting as a health care gadget that monitors users' vital signs to helping blind people navigate roads, or for changing slides in a presentation by tapping their sideburns. A further potential improvement of the wig may use ultrasound waves to detect objects around a user.

Hair accessories that vary from clips to corsages can be used for creating discreet and fashionable gadgets attached to the hair. First Sign Hair Clip [106] is a hair clip with electronics inside that communicates with a mobile application to automatically call for help and collect evidence whenever the user is in danger. The clip detects head impacts associated with a violent crime by using an accelerometer and gyroscope, which automatically triggers the alarm, while a microphone collects evidence.

Designing Hairware

The hair is public as everyone can see it, personal given that it is a body part, and malleable as it suits cultural and personal preferences [107]. This project proposes the use of (modified) artificial hair extensions as a novel wearable technology. We use a chemical platting technique that makes the hair extensions conductive and, at the same time, remains looking like human hair. Then, they are connected to a microcontroller reading sensors or triggering actuators. We use hair clips for attaching the circuit to the hair extensions in order to make them easily removable and replaceable. In addition, this makes it possible to put the circuit in different accessory such as a hairclip, headband, brooch and the top of the hair extensions. This section describes the materials and the prototyping process used. It also shows the feasibility of this technology as both input and output device.

Chemical Process for Creating Hairware

Artificial hair extensions are chemically metalized for acquiring electrical conductivity and keeping a natural coloration. We used six strands of hair extensions of approximately 1.5 by 25 cm each. Before going through the chemical process, they are cleaned and weighted. Tests are performed at DC voltages of 5 V, using a multimeter and a weighing scale.

The chemical process is carried out in two phases: activation and electrolysis. During the first phase, artificial hair extensions, being plastic non-conducting surfaces, require some kind of activation to enable them to be submitted to an electrochemical process. The first activation uses hydrogen and tin chloride. Then, a silver nitrate solution is added for the second activation, where the extensions are set up to catalyze electron transfer reactions, making them ready for metalizing. Next, they are platted by electrolysis. Copper is electrochemically deposited for making them electrically conductive while black nickel gives the natural black effect. A copper plaque is needed for the electrolysis process. Figure 3.10 shows the hair extension during the metalizing process and Table 3.2 shows the formulations and times needed for creating Hairware.

After finishing the chemical process, the hair extensions are weighted. Table 3.3 shows each of the hair extensions initial weight, the final one and the percentage of weight variation. The hair extensions got an average of 21 % more of their original weight. Electrical resistances of each hairpiece are measured with a multimeter, showing that they are highly conductive with a surface resistivity of less than 5 Ω/sq.

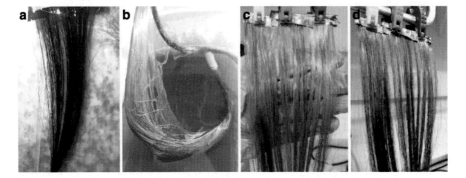

Fig. 3.10 Hair extensions visualizations after the chemical process: (**a**) after Activation 2, (**b**) copper electrolysis, (**c**) copper acid, (**d**) black nickel electrolysis

Table 3.2 Hairware electrochemical process

	Formulation		Temp (°C)	Time (Min)
Activation 1	1 L	Final solution	21	7
	10 g	$SnCl_2$ ($2H_2O$)		
	40 mL	HCl		
Activation 2	1 L	Final solution	21	7
	2 g	$AgNO_3$		
	10 mL	NH_3		
Copper electrolysis	1 L	Final solution	40	10
	14 g	$CuSO_4·5H_2O$		
	30 g	Potassium sodium tartrate ($KNaC_4H_4O_6·4H_2O$)		
	10 g	NaOH		
	40 mL	Formaldehyde (CH_2O)		
Copper acid	1 L	Final solution	21	10
	220 g	$CuSO_4·5H_2O$		
	34 mL	H_2SO_4		
	10 mL	Cupracid solution		
	0.5 mL	Cupracid brightener 210 Part A		
	0.5 mL	Cupracid brightener 210 Part B		
	0.12 g	NaCl		
Black nickel electrolysis	1 L	Final solution	21	10
	120 g	$NiSO_4$		
	40 g	$NiCl_2$		

Table 3.3 Hairware features

	Initial weight (g)	Final weight (g)	Δ Weight (g %)	Resistance (Ω)
Hairware 1	1.35	1.74	22.41	3.8
Hairware 2	1.08	1.16	6.90	4.2
Hairware 3	1.55	1.85	16.22	4.7
Hairware 4	1.34	1.55	13.55	4.8
Hairware 5	0.79	1.17	32.48	4.9
Hairware 6	0.85	1.29	34.11	4.4
	1.16	**1.46**	**20.94**	**4.47**

Hairware as an Output Device

Figure 3.11 shows our first prototype for demonstrating the feasibility of Hairware as an output device. Different kinds of actuators such as buzzers and LEDs are attached to conductive hair extensions to be triggered by a microcontroller [98]. We

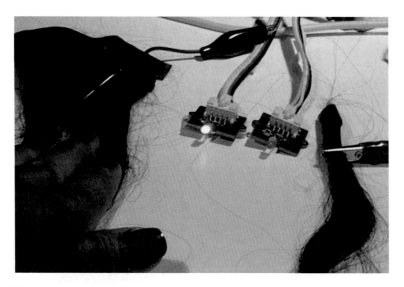

Fig. 3.11 The design of Hairware

connected two Hairware strands to LEDs using hairclips. The positive pin connected to the sender pin on the microcontroller and the negative one grounded. Artificial hair extensions with no conductivity are placed around the conductive hair extensions for isolation. This demo turns on the LEDs attached to the hair and changes their intensity and the lighting effects could mimic the rhythm of the music. Other actuators such as buzzers and vibration motors may replace LEDs.

Hairware as an Input Device

Our first attempts in creating Hairware as an input device were measuring deformation of hair extensions when they were squeezed. In order to learn more about squeezing, we enrolled in the Skweezee workshop at TEI 2014 [96]. There we measured squeeze on deformable objects filled with conductive wool that lowered the object resistance. This approach did not suit this project because Hairware barely changes its resistance when twisted.

In order to show the feasibility of using Hairware as an input device, we used it as a capacitance sensor that detects touch on the extensions. We used an Arduino microcontroller, LEDs, resistors and two Hairware strands. Each of the Hairware strands is connected to a send and receive pin of the microcontroller and two LEDs are also connected to it.

Figure 3.12 shows Hairware's capacitance sensors functionality. When the receiver pin's state change by making a low touch on a strand, the corresponding LED turns on. Thus, each LED is on when this sensor detects that someone is touching Hairware.

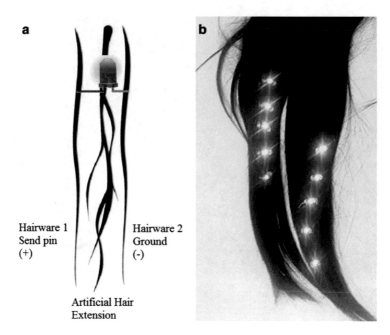

Fig. 3.12 Hairware as an actuator. (**a**) Placing an LED on the conductive hair extensions. (**b**) Lighting Hairware

This circuit creates a pulse delay equivalent to the time that the capacitor takes to charge and discharge. In this way, Hairware plays the part of a conductive surface that detects when another conductive surface touches it. Therefore, given that the human body is conductive and the average internal resistance of the human trunk is ~100 Ω [108], touching Hairware will affect capacitance resulting in a different charging time.

Concealed Interaction

Weiser [50] envisioned a ubiquitous computing paradigm where technology is integrated into everyday experiences in a way that computers vanish into the background. In this way, the major challenge of the Disappearing Computer paradigm [109] is the development of new invisible technologies that fit the task so well that the tool becomes a part of the task [110]. This approach converges in the use of implicit interactions where the user concentrates on her prime goal or targeted activity—tool use is intended, but the user is not actually aware of the interaction with the computer system. In contrast, we propose using explicit interactions meaning that a user operates a system aiming to achieve a certain goal—that is, the user is fully aware of the tool that she is using.

Mainstream research focusses more in creating technologies that users get so used to them that the task becomes invisible rather than investing on the invisibility of the device. Currently, the human body is becoming an important topic in the field of human-computer interaction due to the proximity of wearables to the body combined with the aim of processing user's data in everyday objects. However, there is no doubt that current wearables are nevertheless very distinguishable. On the other hand, recently there have been some efforts in making technology disappear, as is the case with Ringly [47], a gadget in a shape of jewelry that connects to smartphones and gives the user notifications. Ralph Lauren's Polo Tech shirt [48] is another example of seamless fashionable technology that contains conductive silver threads and sensors designed to measure user's performance looking like a classic sport shirt. Moreover, instead of using clothing and accessories, Beauty Technology [75] uses beauty products to hide technology and place them straight on the body surface.

Interactions through gestures and body movements are clearly visible to observers. Gestures are also used for wearable's interactions by touching the wearable in a certain way such as interactions with Google Glass [16], by simulating a known gesture such as Talk to the Hand Project that simulates the gesture of answering a phone [111], and also by creating new gestures such as in the Sixthsense Project [112]. There has being previous exploration using clothes and accessories such as PocketTouch that detects finger-strokes through fabric [113], CheekyWear that mimics a flirting gesture for triggering actions [114] and Cord Input that detects grasping, pulled and twisted gestures on a cord [115]. In contrast, we are proposing an interface that uses the body surface where the nonverbal communication is not straightforwardly decoded. Nonverbal communication modalities might include body motion or kinesics behavior such as facial expression and posture; paralanguage such as laughing and yawning; proxemics; olfaction; skin sensitivity; and the use of objects such as a dress and cosmetics [116]. In this way, most wearables use body motion for sensing gestures. Body motions comprise four types of cues that convey information about the nature and the intensity of an emotion: body acts (clear movements), body positions (non-movement of a body part), facial expressions, and head orientations. [117]. In this project, we used auto-contact behaviors [118], a body act that takes place whenever we touch, stroke or hug ourselves in order to provide comfort, mitigate anxiety or suggest sexual invitation.

This kind of act could also be classified as an adaptor [116] that is triggered by an unconscious feeling that the person rarely intends to communicate and the observer is typically not aware of (Fig. 3.13). In this way, we conceal the interaction with the wearable, creating a concealed interface that consciously makes use of unconscious behaviors (Fig. 3.14). For example, in a social meeting, a user touches the tip of Hairware to make her phone ring, touches the middle to put her phone in mute mode and touches the top to send a pre-customized message to a colleague. In this way, she will continue participating in the meeting and, at the same time, without being noticed, she will be interacting with her phone.

Designing Hairware as an Input Device

Our implementation comprises the hardware and software development of this Beauty Technology. The hardware connects the conductive hair extensions to a circuit. While touching, the software detects on it and identifies the user's intention.

Fig. 3.13 Auto-contact behavior

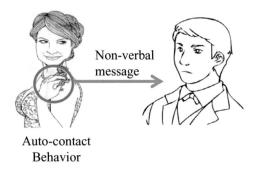

Auto-contact
Behavior

Fig. 3.14 Concealing interaction through Hairware. Photos attribution from *left* to *right*, up to down [119–122]

Hardware

Figure 3.15 shows three layers of non-conductive hair extensions that are added for isolating the hair from the skin. In addition, these layers improved the capacitor sensor values. Each time the user touch the top, middle or tip, the capacitor sensor differentiates these values.

Basically, the circuit compares an output that transmits the pulse and an input that receives the pulse. When a finger touches Hairware, it creates a delay in the pulse, and the microcontroller recalculates this delay. The circuit diagram (Fig. 3.16) comprises four 1 MΩ resistors and one 100 pF capacitor. The resistors select the sensitivity: the bigger the resistor, the farther away it detects a human. With 4 MΩ resistor between the output and input pins, the circuit is tuned to start to respond 1 in. away, just enough

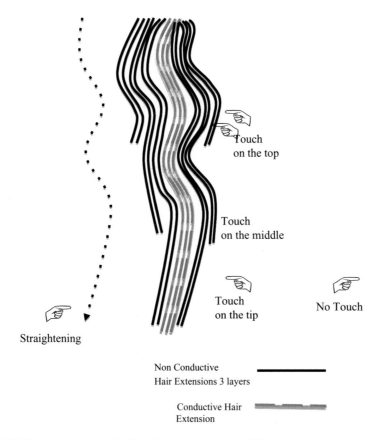

Fig. 3.15 Three layers approach. Changing the capacitance of Hairware by non-conductive artificial hair extensions

to overcome the non-conductive hair layer. The small capacitor (100 pF) placed between the sensor pin and ground improves stability and repeatability. Some LEDs were added to the system to give feedback to the user whenever a touch is detected.

Software

For classification, we use a decision tree implementation provided by BigML [123]. Each transmission from the sensor contains a capacitive charging time in milliseconds, from which we extract for classification. Currently, we can classify five touches interaction in the Hairware: no touch, touch on the top, touch on the middle, touch on tip and straightening.

When trained, the decision tree build an actionable model (Fig. 3.17) that we use as an Arduino function to classify the interaction in real time. Each node represents the confidence action from the read value. The key feature to recognize touch on the hair is not to detect the touch itself, but the circuit must be fine-tuned to detect small capacitance charge variations along the hair.

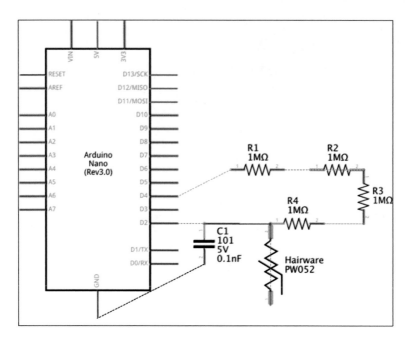

Fig. 3.16 Hairware circuit using Arduino

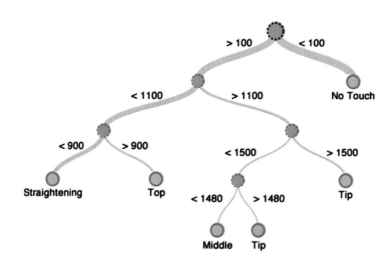

Fig. 3.17 Confidence from the decision tree

Figure 3.18 shows data collected from the five interactions used to classification evaluation. The charts plotted from this data set show the charging time difference from each interaction. As expected the touch on the tip has the higher value because that layer of non-conductive hair is thinner (layer 3). The charging value will decrease

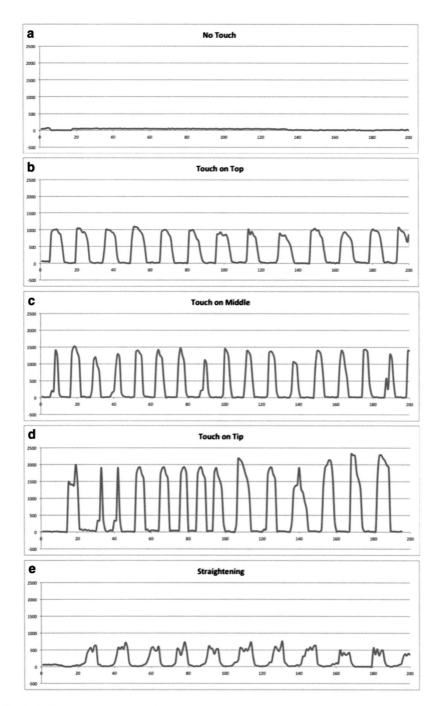

Fig. 3.18 Capacitor sensor values in the different touches (**a**) no touch, (**b**) touch on the *top*, (**c**) touch on the *middle*, (**d**) touch on the *tip*, (**e**) straightening

when the interaction gets near the top where there are more non-conductive hair layers acting as a filter. The straightening actions have the lowest values due to its speed
and skin contact time with the sensor. The "No Touch" graph ranges from 0 to 60
because the hair gets in contact with the human skin without configuring a touch, (no
other touch gets these low results.) "Touch in Top" moves to 1000, "Middle" to
1500, "Tip" to 2200 and "Straightening" to 750. Noise appeared on the readings
given that the hair was in direct contact with the skin. However, our algorithm recognizes it as noise and obtains 92% accuracy on the five trained touch gestures.

Evaluation

For evaluation, we aim to identify the exposure of the technology in Hairware and
we measure the accuracy in replaying the hair straightening, top, middle, and tip
touch. We recruited five female participants, ranging from 28 to 35 in age. We
invited female participants because most of them use or had used long hair, are more
knowledgeable about hair care and its looks and are the ones who do auto-contact
behaviors with their hair. The study took approximately 30 min per participant and
included a gratuity. Given that Hairware is a proof of concept of the technology,
evaluations were done in the same laboratory under the same conditions (temperature, humidity and pressure). We acknowledge that geotemporal factors will affect
the results and a calibration method is required. At the beginning, we conducted
pre-questionnaires to identify the participants' profiles. All participants were right
handed. They had no wearables but were familiar with tablets and smartphones.
None has used a hair extension before but they saw them applied to other girls. All
of them expressed that they touch their hair when they feel anxious, thoughtful and
nervous. Three of them noticed themselves using their hair as a flirting tool.

We interviewed the participants before they observed and used Hairware. We
asked them questions related to Hairware visibility and their familiarity of hair
extensions. While showing Hairware, we asked them their impressions and if they
could identify any differences between these hair extensions and normal or artificial
hair. Then we showed a non-conductive artificial hair extension and asked what differences they could detect between them and Hairware.

After 2 min of training on the different tasks, we asked them to repeat the five
different touches again. They repeated ten times each touch. Figure 3.19 shows the
participant touching the top, middle and bottom part of Hairware during the test.

After the first interview, we identified that, at first sight Hairware was not noticed
as a technological device and they were not aware of its conductivity. Most of the
participants thought they were natural hair extensions and when compared to artificial hair, they noticed that the latter is more shining and has a smoother texture.
They also said that Hairware is not noticeable when attached to someone's hair.

During the tests, we observed that a previous calibration must be done for each
user, in a way that each touch was perceptible by our algorithm. Differences in skin
capacitance and hand position while touching could make the capacitor sensor iden-

Fig. 3.19 Participant testing different touches on Hairware

tify different values for each user. We also notice that other feedback must be designed. LEDs will not be notice if the user is wearing Hairware. We will replace this feedback by vibration motors.

After using Hairware, they said that it was easy to use and that by adding the layers of non-conductive artificial hair extensions gave the device a shiny look and a smooth touch. They said that if the circuit is hidden into the hair or into an accessory, an external observer would not notice the use of Hairware. Future versions of Hairware will also add the touches asked by the participants: twirling their hair and passing the fingers through the head.

During the final interview, participants expressed that they would use Hairware for specific purposes. Most of them recommended using it as a security device. That is, when feeling in danger or being in a risky area, they would like to send a message to the police or to someone they trust without anyone around noticing it. Another suggestion was to use it for triggering house appliances. Another suggestion is to use it as an alarm for stopping dealing with her hair whenever she is continuously doing her nervous tick movement.

We used 80 % of the data of each different touch to train our model and 20 % for testing its accuracy. Then, again, we tested the model with the users to verify whether the touches were being correctly interpreted. The prototype achieved 92 % accuracy on five touch gestures. Hairware was tested in the laboratory under the same conditions. Non-intended gestures and other factors could affect the results and a calibration method would be required. Future work will include an activation gesture such as pressing Hairware for a few seconds. Figure 3.20 shows Hairware's functionalities and the video available at https://youtu.be/13DuvfLzGyE.

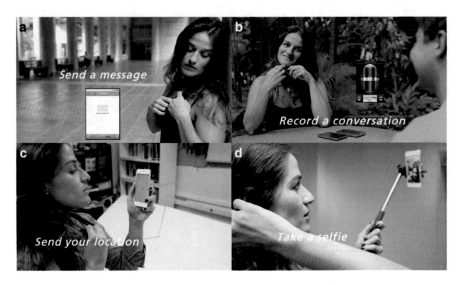

Fig. 3.20 Hairware's functionalities. (**a**) send a message, (**b**) record a conversation, (**c**) send your location, (**d**) take a selfie. Image reproduced with permission from Rejane Matos

Lessons Learned

This project presented Hairware, conductive hair extensions with embedded hardware that can be used as both, input and output device, looking like regular hair extensions. Our approach modified artificial hair extensions into a conductive material using a chemical process. Other materials such as conductive ink and gel hair present conductivity but get easily dried or taken away when touched. Our chemical process can be modified by using other reagents in order to get a different hair coloration. Braids and different hairstyles can be combined in order to keep the hair in a specific position.

We observed that after the copper electrolysis step, the extensions got a golden color. Our aim was to get a darker color thus; we applied the black nickel electrolysis. Nevertheless, the metalizing process could be stopped there for a golden color of the hair extensions and our chemical formulations can be modified with other materials in order to obtain different hair colors.

The hair extensions gained almost 21 % of weight after the chemical process. However, we observed that this is not a noticeable weight for such a slight device. Although most of the hair threads were very conductive, a higher resistance turned up at some hair threads (about 120 Ω) from the top to the tip of the hair.

Due to skin conductivity, Hairware should be placed on any non-conductive material, a shirt for example, for isolating it from the skin. Moreover, other conductive materials like jewelry could affect the way it operates. Future work will include a new step in our chemical process that will isolate all conductive hair extensions preserving their capacitance.

Hairware should be connected to a circuit that can be placed at the base of the hair extension, in an earring, necklace and hairclip. Due to the proximity of Hairware to the head, vibration motors can be included in order to give feedback to the user. Future work will add an isolation material at the end of the process so users will not need to have a direct contact with the conductive material. When used as an output device, other actuators such as vibration motors and buzzers may replace LEDs. When used as an input device, it can be combined with other wearables such as glasses, brain waves and conductive makeup. Other materials such as beards and mustaches can be transformed into conductive materials and other techniques may be explored like the use of conductive polymers.

Our approach for using Hairware as an input device based on human gestures is seamless, and the gestures that trigger other devices could remain unnoticed by an external observer. In this way, depending on how Hairware is used, there are some controversial concerns related to privacy that are controversial. For example, a Hairware user could start recording a conversation without asking authorization from the observer.

We used Hairware as an input device that consciously used unconscious auto-contact behaviors to trigger different devices such as a TV set, home appliances and smartphones. We envision the use of Hairware in situations that the interaction is intended to be hidden such as in certain meetings, for secret agents and for magicians. Moreover, Hairware may explore the different meanings of hair in terms of culture and emotions by figuring out levels of stress and anxiety whenever the user touches her hair. In addition, as hair is generally a focus of women, Hairware would be used for calling for protection in risky situations. In this way, it could be used as an alarm device that sends messages informing the user's location. Adding an Radio Frequency IDentification (RFID) and other sensors to it, it will possible to provide more evidence to the court of law and the police.

Chapter 4
Skin Interfaces

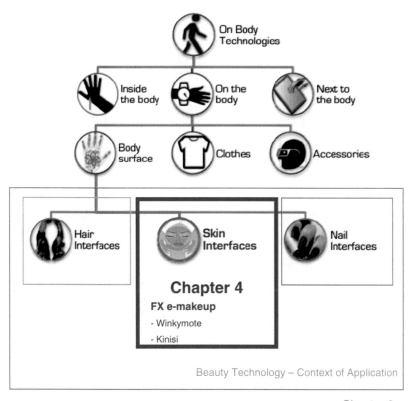

Fig. 4.1 Chapter 4: Skin interfaces

© Springer International Publishing Switzerland 2016
K. Vega, H. Fuks, *Beauty Technology*, Human–Computer Interaction Series,
DOI 10.1007/978-3-319-15762-7_4

Interfaces on the Skin

Wearable electrochemical sensors are being massively deployed for healthcare [124]. Advances in this technology when integrated into clothing could be considered as non-invasive. However, they are not easily attachable for extracting bio data [125]. Temporary Transfer Tattoo [126] are electrodes printed directly on the epidermis by dispersing carbon fiber segments within the tattoo ink. A true integration with wearables and an attractive way of hiding sensors is expected using these electrodes designed as an artistic tattoo.

Mc10 are proposing smart sensing stickers for medicine, therapy and healthcare in a bandage-like device [127]. They print an electronic mesh onto a flexible thin plastic that is malleable and adaptable to the human skin as a removable tattoo in order to read brain waves, heart, muscle, body temperature and motion, and even hydration levels.

Although privacy and health issues are currently being debated, wearers nevertheless seize the opportunity to experiment with the sensation of being injected with tiny electronic devices. They are also looking for new experiences and fashion, like tattoo implants that use the skin as a display [126] and chipping humans with RFID tag implants to track people's comings and goings [128, 129]. In the Arts field there are some efforts too, placing LEDs close to the eyes simulating larger eyes [23] and acting as glowing eye shadows when the eyes are closed [130].

FX e-makeup

Previous Beauty Technology prototypes attach seamless sensors on the user's face by using Conductive Eyelashes to act as blinking switches. In this project, we propose FX e-makeup, another Beauty Technology that is focused on the human agency for controlling devices by sensing voluntary movements of facial muscles. It differs from: Computational Vision that provides methods for facial expression analysis by automatically recognizing facial motions and facial feature changes from visual information [131]; Bio-potential sensors such as EEG, EMG, and EOG that have been used as inputs for several healthcare devices [131]; and Brain-Computer Interfaces that link the computer to the human nervous and muscular system for recognition of user's gestures in several hands free interfaces [132–134].

Interfaces for Sensing Facial Actions

In past decades, significant effort has been made in developing techniques for sensing facial expressions [135] that originate in the muscles under the skin of the face. Involuntary movements convey the emotional state of an individual to observers through nonverbal communication.

Micro movements involve facial muscle actions that are triggered by nerve impulses generated by emotions. Maximally Discriminative Facial Movement Coding System (MAX) [136] and Facial Action Coding System (FACS) [137] are observational coding systems for identifying micro movements thought to be associated with emotion. All possible facial displays are coded in 44 action units that represent an individual's muscles movement [138]. Traditionally, FACS' measurements are done by experts' observation [139]. However, thanks to advances in technology, there are other techniques that support recognition of action units like Computational Vision techniques, which senses movements and gestures and reproduces them in a 3D environment [140].

When humans initiate a voluntary action, the brain sends an electrochemical signal that traverses our nervous system through the spinal cord and eventually reaches the motor neurons. They stimulate specific muscles causing movement or force [137]. Non-vision techniques for identifying voluntary actions include EMG that measures the potential difference between two muscles. There are some known issues associated with using EMG [138] such as the placement of leads on the face inhibiting the movements of the subject, ambiguities in the measurements due to the proximity of the muscles and lack of specific places to attach the electrodes. Several devices make use of EMG such as a head-mounted measurement device that senses the intensity of facial activity [141]. The muscles responsible for raising the eyebrows, lowering the eyebrows, raising the mouth corners, and pulling down the mouth corners are measured simultaneously using a capacitive method and EMG. The artist Manabe uses electric sensors to stimulate muscles in his face in synchronization with music [142]. Another example is the Tongue Computer Interface that was developed for patients with paralyzing injuries or medical conditions. Infrared optical sensors are embedded within a dental retainer in order to sense explicit tongue movements [143].

FX e-makeup Design

The senses of agency and of body ownership are two aspects in the bodily self that must be distinguished to identify different effects in body awareness [144]. A person has the capacity to act in the world through his sense of agency. Thus, intending and executing actions include the feeling of controlling one's own body movements, and, through them, events in the external environment [140]. Only voluntary actions produce a sense of agency that is originated in neural processes responsible for the motor aspects of action [145]. On the other hand, the sense of body ownership refers to the understanding that the person's own body is the source of her movements or sensations, whether voluntary or not [146]. During a voluntary action, sensor mechanisms generate a sense of body ownership, thus, the unity of bodily self-consciousness comes from action and not from sensation [147]. In this project, we propose an interface that makes use of the sense of agency inherent in humans to augment their capacities through voluntary muscle movements.

The muscles of the face are divided into two groups according to their function: expressive or mimetic muscles and mastication muscles (four muscles attached to the bone and ligament that are mainly used for chewing and have a minor effect on expression) [147]. Facial expressions are caused by the movement of the mimetic muscles that are attached to the skin and fascia in the face, unlike other skeletal muscles that are attached to the bones. These groups of muscles move the skin, creating lines, folds and wrinkles, causing the movement of facial features, such as mouth and eyebrows [147]. FX e-makeup sensors act as switches when strategically placed on these muscles.

Duchenne de Boulogne [148] found that some muscles that are activated by emotions are difficult to activate voluntarily. Ekman et al. [149] also addresses the same difficulty in voluntary movements but got different results when children were asked to voluntarily activate muscular actions by imitating a model presented on a video monitor. The Gosselin Report [150], based on Facial Action Code System (FACS), determines the extent to which adults are able to voluntarily produce facial muscular actions and to discover the muscles that can be activated without the co-activation of other unwanted muscles. Twenty participants were asked to produce 20 facial action units, reproducing each action five times. Figure 4.2 indicates the percentage of participants who were able to activate the target action units at least once [150].

Based on this report, we identified the action units that are used in our study. FACS' action units plus combinations that achieved more than 95 % of success (except for the lip presser that achieved roughly 75 % of success) and had fewer associations with other movements are the ones that are considered in this project: jaw drop, lips part, lip corner puller, lid tighten, outer low brow raiser and lip pressor. Jaw drop and lips part action units had no associated movements. The lip corner puller action unit is associated with the check raiser action unit and the outer brow raiser is associated with the inner brow raiser one: in both cases, the associated movement is not constantly repeated. The chin raiser was the action unit most associated with other movements (five times). The lower lip depressor has the chin raiser action unit as an associated movement. Both action units were discarded. The lid tighten action unit achieved 95 % of success and got the lowest percent of associated movements. Figure 4.3 shows sensors applied to the muscles relevant to this project.

FX e-makeup Prototypes

Kinisi and Winkymote are the prototypes that show FX e-makeup feasibility.

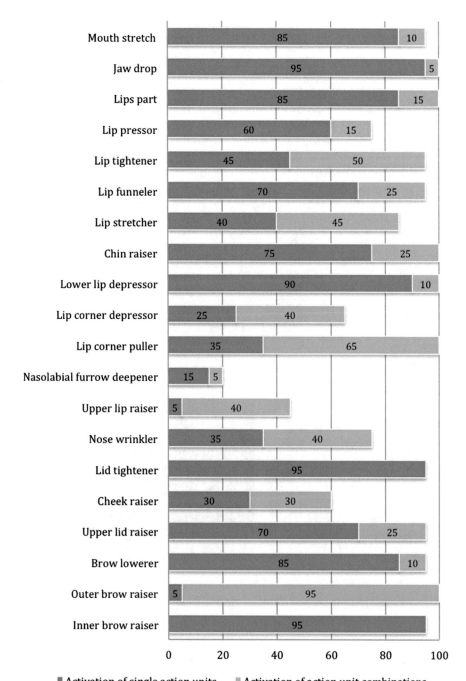

Fig. 4.2 G1: Percentage of participants who succeeded in activating the target action units [150]

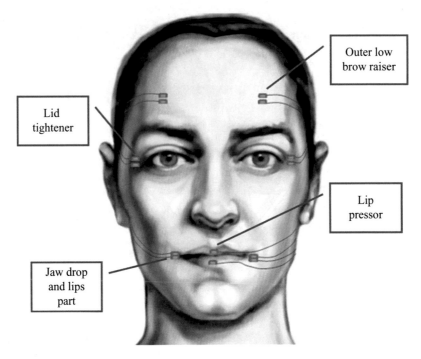

Fig. 4.3 FX e-makeup interface. Sensors connected to muscles

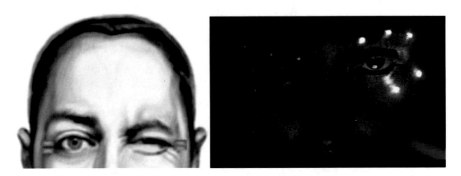

Fig. 4.4 Eyelid sensor. Image reproduced with permission from Gabriella Chávez

Kinisi

Sensors are connected using the FX makeup. Figure 4.4 shows the eyelid sensor (associate with the lid tightener action unit) that senses blinking when the lid is tightener and the contacts touch each other. Figure 4.5 shows the sensor located on the brow, associated with the outer low brow raiser action unit, that is activated when the user raises her eyebrow and the contacts touch each other. The sensor on Fig. 4.6 is associated with the

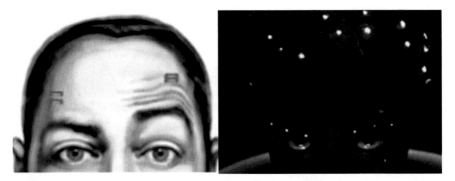

Fig. 4.5 Eyebrow sensor. Image reproduced with permission from Gabriella Chávez

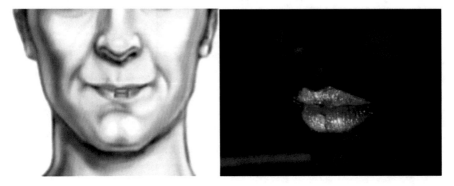

Fig. 4.6 Closing lips sensor. Image reproduced with permission from Gabriella Chávez

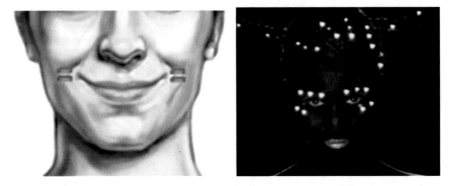

Fig. 4.7 Smile sensor. Image reproduced with permission from Gabriella Chávez

lip pressor action unit that activates when both lips are pressed together. Finally, Fig. 4.7 shows the sensor associated with the Jaw drop, lips part, and lip corner puller action units. It senses a smile when there is no contact, in the opposite way to the other sensors. Wires are hidden using FX makeup materials like ink and latex. Figure 4.8 shows the schematics with the sensors and the LED strings that are activated.

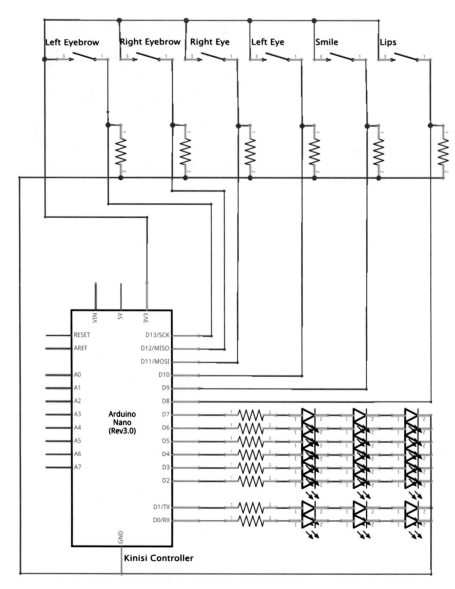

Fig. 4.8 Kinisi circuit schematics

Kinisi tries to answer the following question: "Can your skin act as an interface?" by activating different light patterns with smiles, winks, raised eyebrows and
closing lips [151]. The voluntary movements approximate the two points closing
the circuit. Depending on the shape of the face, action units are identified and
marked as it is shown in Fig. 4.9. Firstly, a layer of latex is applied to the skin in
order to isolate it from the electronics. Sensors are precisely glued to the latex mask
on the chosen points. LEDs are placed on the mask and between braids. Finally, face

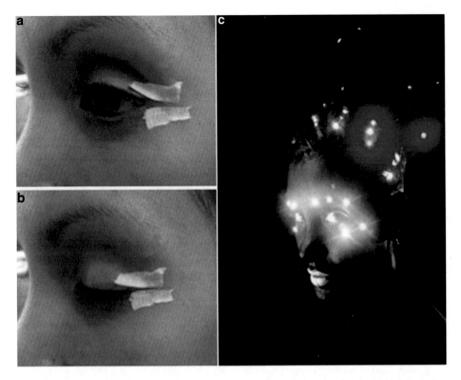

Fig. 4.9 Kinisi. (**a**) eyelid in a neutral position, (**b**) eyelid up closing the circuit, (**c**) kinisi wearing FX e-makeup. Image reproduced with permission from Gabriella chávez

paint is used to color the user's face black. The Kinisi video was showed in Beauty Technology's presentations and in the Digital Futures exhibition (Annex 2). A video is available at https://youtu.be/7JrRo1U7c5o.

Winkymote

Numerous approaches have been tried to develop technological solutions to facilitate independent communication and mobility for individuals with disabilities, among these the mouth stick, sensors activated by blinking, respiration and head movement [152, 153]. A communication interface controlled by voluntary blinking that activates infrared controlled devices simulating a remote control is being developed for individuals with quadriplegic disability.

Felipe, a 33-year-old M.Sc. administration student, inspired Winkymote. He hurt himself playing jujitsu and at publication time has had quadriplegic disability for 14 years. Felipe uses a speech recognition system keyboard replacement to control his computer but, unfortunately, depends on others to do common activities such as changing television channels.

Fig. 4.10 Winkymote, an infrared-controlled interface for individuals with quadriplegic disability

Winkymote (Fig. 4.10) is an infrared-controlled interface that uses FX e-makeup sensors connected to an infrared-transmitting module mounted on the user's necklace. These sensors are placed close to the outer end of each eye, i.e., close to the lid tighten action unit. They are connected through wires to the infrared-transmitting module mounted on his chest. Whenever he winks tightly, the switch closes sending a digital signal to the microcontroller that vibrates as feedback to inform an infrared LED that it is sending the appropriate sequences for triggering the television. Blinking with his left or right or both eyes turns the television on, off or changes the channels up and down. Figure 4.11 shows the circuit schematic that includes the sensors for both eyes, the infrared emitter and the vibrator motor for the feedback. Figure 4.12 shows the evaluation application of Winkymote and Felipe using and turning on the TV for the first time by himself after 13 years.

Lessons Learned

The first FX e-makeup prototype comprised gelatin powder without flavor, distilled water and glycerin. This kind of FX makeup is often used for creating prosthetics such as wounds, scars, burns and blisters. Finding the proper makeup consistency depends on preparation given that it requires heating the ingredients. Our initial results were too thick and had the tendency to fall off depending on the skin properties and the user's movements. Three participants wore the makeup for 6 h. However, it did not work on Felipe, whose makeup fell off after 1 h, due to his oily skin. After deciding to use hydrogel, which helped fix the electronics, we had to give up for the same reason: his oily skin (Fig. 4.13). Finally, we tried liquid latex. It was applied to the skin using a disposable sponge taking about

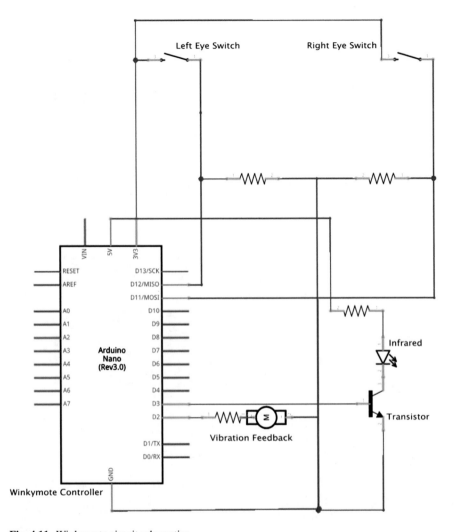

Fig. 4.11 Winkymote circuit schematics

5 min to dry. As it dried, it turned to a rubbery consistency and was molded to his face. Then, more layers were applied to the skin in order to embed and isolate the electronic components.

The face has over 40 anatomically independent muscles referred to as specific action units that could be co-activated. The corrugator muscle group, for instance, which brings the brows down and together, consist of three muscles that are normally activated together. Although, the sensors on the FX e-makeup action units could operate independently, not all combinations are possible like concurrently raising the left eyebrow and tightening the left eyelid, and raising each eyebrow independently.

Fig. 4.12 Winkymote usage. (**a**) placing sensors on skin, (**b**) connecting the remote control. (**c**) first time Felipe turn on the TV by himself after 13 years. Image reproduced with permission from Felipe Esteves

Action units' activation differs in duration and intensity. In contrast to previous prototypes on Conductive Makeup where a preset time interval for sensing voluntary movements was defined, given that FX e-makeup sensors are precisely located, they are only activated when the intensity of the movement reaches its maximum.

Fig. 4.13 Winkymote first
prototype using hydrogel

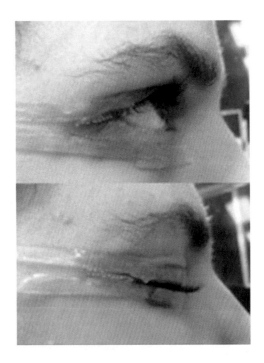

FX e-makeup may be used to control multiple devices. Sensors could be connected to a variety of devices providing user feedback and communication with other devices. For example, a wearable for changing slides (closing the right eye the presentation moves forward to the next slide) was developed to work with Winkymote.

Future work will include new Beauty Technologies to sense other facial action units via FX e-makeup. Sensors and their duration/intensity level combinations connected to other action units will be incorporated to FX e-makeup prototypes. We also intend to expand FX e-makeup sensors to explore neck movements for controlling different devices like air conditioning and hospital beds. Other future potential uses of this technology will explore novel hands free interfaces like dealing with amplifying or unnoticed gestures, keeping people awake, and decoding blinking gestures for physical and physiological analysis.

Chapter 5
Nail Interfaces

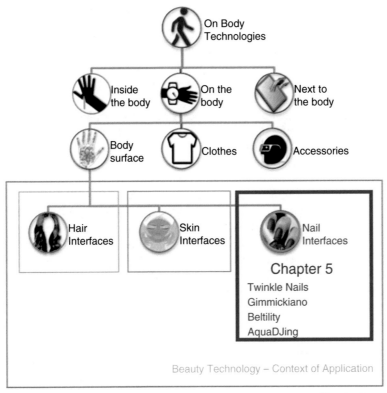

Fig. 5.1 Chapter 5: Nail interfaces

© Springer International Publishing Switzerland 2016
K. Vega, H. Fuks, *Beauty Technology*, Human–Computer Interaction Series,
DOI 10.1007/978-3-319-15762-7_5

Interfaces on Fingertips

Differently from many projects that present finger gesture recognition through cameras and Microsoft Kinect, this project focuses its analysis on wearables that are always available and mobile features. Fingertips are in direct contact with objects that humans interact with and finger muscles are finely controlled by our motor system. Thus, nail displays, rings with embedded electronics and magnetic sensors bracelets have been developed for mobile and ubiquitous interactions (Fig. 5.1).

Nail mounted displays are one example of a wearable that augment reality by providing a visual feedback to the wearer [154]. NailDisplay is an OLED display coupled with sensors atop a fingernail [155]. When the finger is placed on the smartphone screen, the nail display augments its visualization. It also has sensors for identifying pressing and shaking motions. Fingernail Displays [156] envisions the use of a nail polish that automatically configures itself to an active matrix color display.

Finger-worn devices embed several sensors for gesture recognition. FingerRing [157] places rings coupled with accelerometers on every finger for sensing different chord gestures in order to be used as a wearable keyboard. Pingu [158], a ring that detects motion by using accelerometers and gyroscopes, and orientation by using magnetometers.

Another technique for recognizing gestures is by tracking hand motion. An object that has a magnetic sensor recognizes a magnet located on any finger. Neya [159] is a tracking bracelet that detects the 1D input of a strong magnetic ring and communicates wirelessly with other devices. Likewise, Abracadabra [160] uses a magnet on the fingertip to control a wristwatch.

Hinckley [161] identifies these three characteristics of several input devices. Several touch input devices recognize user's fingers that are in contact with the object. For example, Microsoft Surface recognizes which finger is making contact with the laptop [162]. Input devices could differentiate between users. DiamondTouch [163] differentiates users' touch using a surface that generates location dependent electric fields. Computer vision techniques are also being used for user identification and to distinguish finger differentiation [161].

Beauty Tech Nails with RFIDs

The design of wearables involves both knowledge of the human body and electronics. Due to the development of hardware, it is possible to place electronic components on the body as they are getting smaller and more powerful. However, human factors do not change that fast: fingers retain the same size and shape. Even more, the interaction with objects through fingernails such as a piano, a keyboard and any press-and-play object through a sequence of finger movements remains the same. The same could be said regarding the motor learning skills that humans had to gain with their fingers in order to interact with specific targets [164]. In addition, finger based interactions tend to be faster than interaction based on other body parts. Experiments compared interactions using different body parts as input devices: fingers, wrist, arm [165]. They demonstrate that the motor cortex is highly devoted to muscles groups like fingers. These findings determine that finger based input devices have a promising chance to succeed.

The major challenge that wearable input devices are facing today is to ensure that they are unobtrusive [166]. Aforementioned related works show different finger-worn interfaces where batteries, wires and circuits are exposed and, therefore, they are not accepted as everyday objects. On the other hand, Beauty Tech Nails are fake nails that hide electronics like RFID tags, small magnets and conductive polish enabling the wearer to interact with objects in the environment.

RFID Based Interaction

The wide adoption of RFID systems creates opportunities for new and innovative services. It enables organizations to deliver value-added applications related to the tracking and intelligent management of anything tagged with an RFID tag [167]. RFID tags fall into two categories: Active tags are read/write devices that require a power supply, while passive tags are generally read-only devices. Passive tags draw their power from the reader through inductive coupling that requires close proximity. Beauty Tech Nails RFID tags fall in the latter category by using an RFID glass-capsule-tag embedded into each fake nail. A 32-bit non-reprogrammable unique ID that works at 125 KHz frequency is used. The RFID reader [168] recognizes a tag within about 2 cm of distance as it is shown in Fig. 5.2. We chose this short distance reader due to the interspaces between fingers and their motion possibilities, because,

Fig. 5.2 Interaction between beauty tech nail and the reader

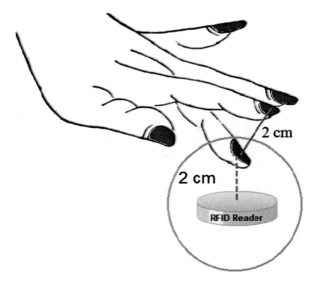

whenever a specific finger is interacting with the reader, this finger is the only one on the reader's range and there is a space between fingers of about 2 cm. Using a long distance reader, all Beauty Tech Nails are recognized rendering them useless.

The main advantages of using RFID systems are the non-contact and non-line-of-sight characteristics of the technology. Tags detectable in a variety of visually and environmentally challenging conditions such as snow, ice, fog, paint, grime, inside containers and vehicles and even inside storage [169]. A specific advantage of passive tags is that they are very small and do not require batteries or maintenance, having an indefinite operational life.

Tech Nails Design

The chosen RFIDs' dimensions are 12.25 mm width by 1.93 mm in diameter. They are hidden either into plastic/acrylic gel sandwich nails or into salon gel nails. The former are easily attached and removed using common glue for fake plastic nails. In this case, tags are sandwiched between the fake plastic nails and the acrylic gel.

Gel nails are a type of artificial nail that most closely resembles natural nails. They could be kept on fingers for more than 5 weeks. The gel is applied to nails in several thinly layers, with each layer being cured under a UV lamp for about 2 min. After it dries, tag is placed on the top of the basecoat after it dries. After that, several thin gel layers are applied until they completely cover the RFID. A decorative design using nail polish is applied to hide the RFID at the end of the process. Figure 5.3 shows this process.

Interactive Possibilities and Prototypes

In this section, Beauty Tech Nails prototypes are presented. They embed RFID tags into fake nails and take advantage of the RFID possibilities for presenting different interactions: non-contact interaction, unusual interactions, and wearables interaction.

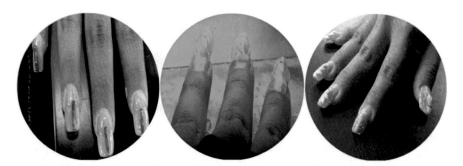

Fig. 5.3 Prototyping beauty tech nails. Gel nail process. Step 1. RFID tag placed on the top of the dried basecoat gel, step 2. curing gel layers, step 3. decorative nail design

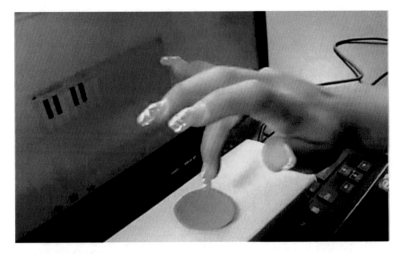

Fig. 5.4 Twinkle nails, non-contact piano playing on a computer

Non-contact Interaction

Using the RFID's proximity feature, the fingernail does not need to touch the smart object to identify it. Whenever the finger is closer than 2 cm from the reader, its unique ID is recognized. Twinkle Nails is a musical combo comprising a Beauty Tech Nail and a box hiding a RFID reader that translates each ID tag into a different note (Fig. 5.4). The video is available at https://youtu.be/J-nTveVvM9U.

The first version of Twinkle nails is a box connected directly to a computer. The box hides an RFID reader that translates into musical notes played by the computer and it displays an interactive piano. The second version was used for exhibitions. A new box hides LEDs and a speaker that turn on when the reader (connected to an Arduino) detects an RFID nail (Fig. 5.5). Figure 5.6 shows the circuit schematics of Twinkle Nails.

Interactions from Tech Nails to Wearables

RFID readers are also embedded into wearable to add extra mobility, which is the case with Gimmickiano (Fig. 5.7) and Beltility (Fig. 5.8). The former, is a wearable piano belt that a performer wears while she moves around the auditorium. The wearable sends the notes to the computer through a radio module, and when she approximates each nail to her belt, the notes are played, and displayed as a piano visualization.

Beltility is a wearable belt that senses each of the Tech Nails and associates it with a specific function on a computer such as moving forward on the slideshow, moving backwards, turn up the volume and turn it down. It includes an RFID reader

Fig. 5.5   Twinkle nails version 2, non-contact piano playing on a musical box

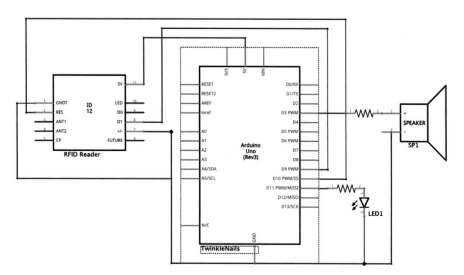

Fig. 5.6   Twinkle nails circuit schematics

connected to a radio module that sends the tags to another radio that is connected to the computer. When the computer receives known tags, it triggers it functionality. A vibration motor is connected to the reader for giving feedback each time a tag is recognized. Figure 5.9 shows the user wearing Beltility. Figure 5.10 shows Beltility circuit's design.

Fig. 5.7 Gimmickiano, wearable that recognizes RFID nails. Image reproduced with permission from Maribel Tafur

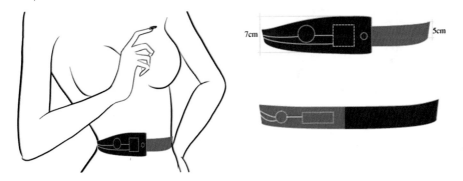

Fig. 5.8 Beltility design

Unusual Interactions

An RFID reader is able to detect tags through different materials like water, glass and wood and also through different states of matter like ice and vapour. AquaDJing makes use of Beauty Tech Nails to interact through water. RFID nails are detected without touching the "DJ Controller" that is sitting at the bottom of a water container. The DJ's performance mixes tracks and sound effects by touching the water. When the reader detects an RFID, the controller selects if it is a group or a track and send it to the computer. LEDs are turn on under the aquarium in order to send a visual feedback to the DJ. Figure 5.11 shows the schematics of AquaDJing. The controller is connected to a computer that has two screens. The first one is presented to the public and shows visualizations

Fig. 5.9 Beltility being used in a presentation

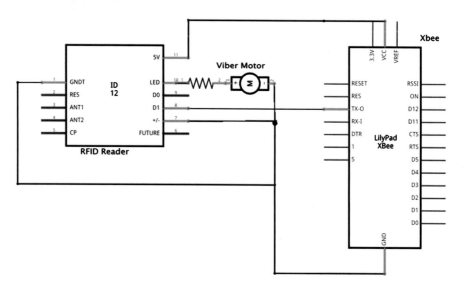

Fig. 5.10 Beltility circuit schematics

animated by the music. The second one is the DJ visualization of the track and sound effect that is being played (Fig. 5.12). A video is available at https://youtu.be/HliI8SGBc2U.

AquaDJing project was used by DJ Maribel Tafur at Telefónica (Lima), Opera singer Elen Nas at Mostra PUC under the project Sentido Aware (Rio de Janeiro), DJ Congo Sanchez from Thievery Corporation at the Women 2.0 Conference (Las Vegas), DJ Sankha at Wear + D (D.F. Mexico) and DJ Kirin at Make it Wearables Intel (San Francisco). Figure 5.13 shows them using AquaDJing.

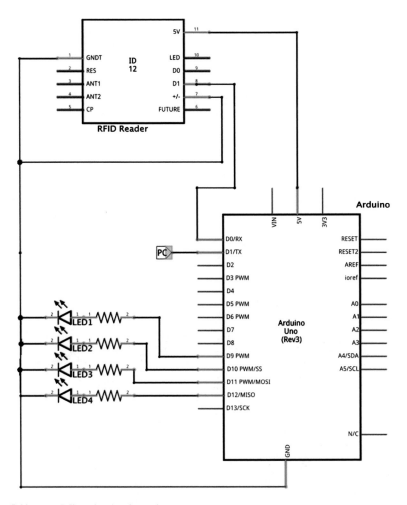

Fig. 5.11 AquaDJing circuit schematics

This was an iterative development with new/modified features added for each presentation. In the first presentation, 25 tracks were played. On her left hand, she controls the group number that is activated and in the right one, the individual tracks to be played. Thus, when she activates the group number 2 (second fingernail on her left hand), she can activate the five tracks in this group with her right hand (from tracks six to ten). Groups 1, 2 and 3 were the tracks, and Groups 4 and 5 were sound effects. When a new track is activated, the last track stops and the new track is played. When a sound effect is activated, it is played once over the track without stopping it. The first and second screen shows a music equalizer.

An opera singer performed the second presentation. She needed just one track to be activated and all the other 24 combinations were sound effects. In this way, she added new water sound effects while the main track is played and

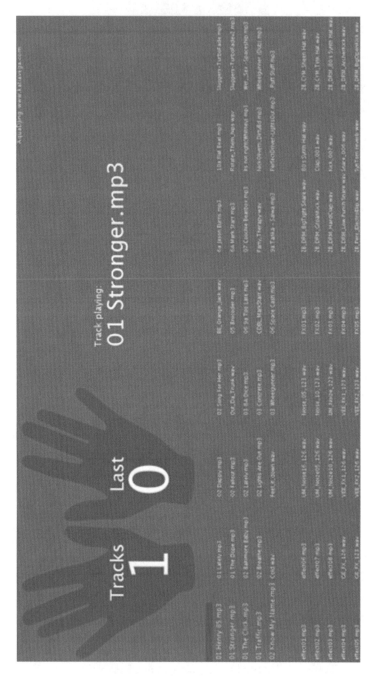

Fig. 5.12 AquaDJing, DJ visualization of tracks and sound effects

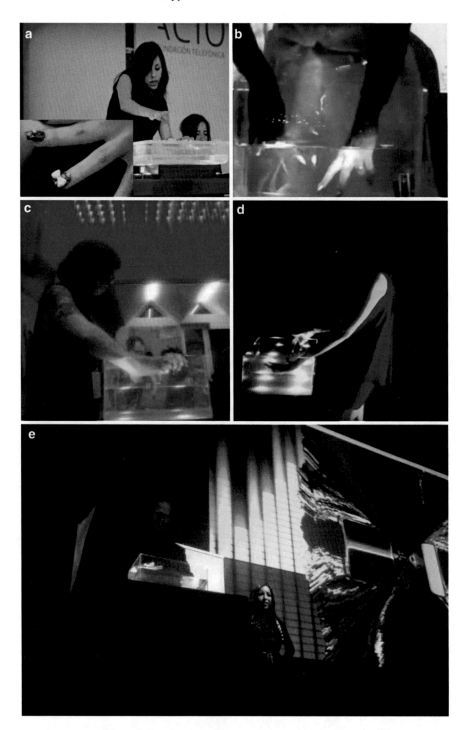

Fig. 5.13 AquaDJing, mixing tracks touching water surface. (**a**) DJ Maribel Tafur, (**b**) Sentido Aware, Opera singer playing tracks and sound effects touching into the water, (**c**) DJ Kirin Rider, (**d**) DJ Sankha, (**e**) DJ Congo Sanchez. Image reproduced with permission from the DJs

she sings. The third presentation was based on the first development with new music visualizations. In addition, one of the combinations stopped all the music. The nails were painted with black polish for the male DJ. The fourth presentation differentiates the second screen for giving feedback to the DJ, showing the name of the track that is played and a list of her music tracks and sound effects. In the fifth presentation, 80 tracks were played. The left hand continued controlling the groups, but now, the DJ can activate the tracks' groups going to the next one each time she uses the first fingernail and going back with her second fingernail. The sound effects groups were activated in the same way using the third and fourth fingernail. The Fifth fingernail stopped the music. It also changed the DJ screen. It showed two hands, the left hand with the group that is activated and the right hand with the track or sound effect that was played. All the tracks and sound effects are shown as lists and the active group is highlighted. Figure 5.12 shows this screen.

Lessons Learned

The advantages of using low frequency RFID tags were appropriate in order to create interactive prototypes with Beauty Tech Nails. They are fashionable, wireless and always on without needing to be connected to batteries. A small glass capsule RFID tag is protected for everyday use by acrylic gel in plastic nails and by salon gel in gel nails. These tags need no contact for tag detection and recognition even when interacting through different materials and states of matter. Short distance passive tag readers make use of the interspaces between fingers for disambiguating targets. This technology identifies individual fingers motion, thus constituting a different sub-area of gesture recognition.

Wearables and smart objects were created to interact with Beauty Tech Nails. Prototypes for displaying non-touch interaction (Twinkle Nails), interacting in unusual conditions like through the water (AquaDJing) and adding extra mobility when interacting with wearables (Gimmickiano) were developed.

Future Beauty Tech Nails will combine low and high frequency RFID tags, magnets and conductive nail polish. As the miniaturization of sensors, batteries and other electromagnetic components evolve, they will be added to new Beauty Tech Nails versions. These nails will interact with a variety of different smart objects on the Internet of Things. Future prototypes may substitute known input devices for Beauty Tech Nails adding new kinds of interactions to their repertoire.

Chapter 6
Final Consideration

Due to the acceptance and daily use of beauty products, electronic components were embedded into them for transforming the body into an interactive computing platform. Wearables are taking on a more essential role in our daily lives, making possible other forms of communication and computing. This project presented our approach on using the human body as an interactive platform, introducing Beauty Technology as a subfield in Wearable Computing.

Traditional beauty products are used for beautifying, promoting attractiveness, altering the appearance and cleansing. They are easy to apply and remove, and are ergonomically designed for the human body. This project adapts beauty products by embedding electronics in order to extend the uses of beauty products, increasing wearers' possibilities for interacting with other devices and being part of the Internet of Things.

Wearables are traditionally placed on clothes and accessories, but following our approach, they placed directly on the surface of the body. We proposed a classification of on body technologies for identifying our application context. In this way, our prototypes were placed on the hair, nails and skin.

Wearables are improving the way they respond to a wide range of human inputs. We analyzed micro and macro body movements to propose technologies that react to voluntary movements. The micro movements sensed were the facial expressions of blinking, smiling, raising eyebrows and closing lips by the Conductive Makeup and FX e-makeup prototypes. Beauty Tech Nails and Hairware sensed finger movements and the touching of the hair that are related to the Arm/hand macro movements, respectively.

Although minimizing awareness while interacting with technology continues to be an important guideline in Ubiquitous Computing, our concern regarding the Invisible Computing Paradigm is that users are not consciously aware that these pieces of technology are gathering and processing data. In contrast, we propose interactions that the user is consciously aware of and intends to generate them, though in a concealed way, by enacting auto-contact behaviors. Thus, the invisibility of the interaction is not hidden to the user but it is hidden to the observer.

© Springer International Publishing Switzerland 2016
K. Vega, H. Fuks, *Beauty Technology*, Human–Computer Interaction Series,
DOI 10.1007/978-3-319-15762-7_6

This project presented an exploration between the body surface, technology and interaction. Consequently, its prototypes were created in an interdisciplinary fashion. Design, chemistry, body structure, human behavior, electronics and software were the basis for creating this technology; opening new research possibilities in several areas.

Wearable Computing offers a variety of functionalities depending on the purpose. Beecham Research Report identified wearable products spread in the sectors of business operations, security, medical, wellness, fitness, lifestyle computing, communication and glamor [170]. Next section shows this classification applied to Beauty Technology.

Beauty Technologies by Sectors

In this chart, seven sectors are identified: security/safety, medical, wellness, sport/fitness, lifestyle computing, communication and glamor. Figure 6.1 shows the Beauty Technology Application chart, based on Beecham's sectors for Wearable Technologies.

Glamor Sector

The Glamor sector includes applications aimed at highlighting the body appearance and using makeup for making a fashion statement. This includes decorative display, light embellishment, interactive performance and emotional response on cosmetics such as art projects and conceptual videos that show the feasibility of these technologies. Table 6.1 shows this sector's applications and its relation with Beauty Technology.

Blinklifier uses Conductive Makeup to amplify the model's blinking using an artistic headdress that has a microprocessor and an LED matrix that makes changes in light patterns [171]. In the case of Arcana, music and images visualizations are created based on the actress's blinking [75]. Superhero also uses Conductive Makeup to communicate the wearer's blinking, changing the environment in ways such as shifting displayed images and even, levitating an object [96]. Tech Nails are decorated fake nails with embedded RFIDs [76]. Twinkle Nails is an application of Tech Nails that is used for playing a piano without having to touch any object. AquaDjing is a DJ music controller device that is operated through water using Tech Nails. Kinisi uses FX e-makeup for triggering different light patterns on the actress's hair and face when she smiles, raises her eyebrow, blinks and closes her lips [78]. LED Eyelashes exemplify the desire of Asian girls of having bigger eyes by turning on LEDs around her eyes [23]. Lumi Deco Nails

Fig. 6.1 Beauty technologies by sectors

Table 6.1 Glamor sector

Applications	Functions	Products and prototypes
Light embellishment	Fashion through lights	Lumi Deco [77], LED eyelashes [23]
Decorative display	Display touch	e-Pannosa [172]
Emotional response	Amplify emotions	Blinkifier, Arcana [95] Kinisi [78]
Interactive performances	Playful show	AquaDJing, Twinkle Nails [76]

are fingernails with NFC tags and LEDs that light up when touching a smartphone [77]. e-Pannosa is a cream applied to the skin that will emit light particles caused by the body's friction [172].

Communication Sector

The Communication sector includes applications related to interacting with other people, like group interaction through social media and physical expression [170]. Common functionalities in this sector are made through wireless communication to connected devices such as using a smartphone in order to have access to voice, text and email; to interact through social media; and to use touch such a hug or a kiss to trigger devices. Table 6.2 shows this sector's applications and its relation with Beauty Technology.

iSkin [79] is a flexible sensor in a shape of a tattoo that recognizes touch on the body. It can be used for controlling and answer in a smartphone when someone calls. Hairware [99] uses conductive hair extensions for sending messages via a smartphone. One possible Hairware application is to call the police or send a message to the family or friends asking for help in risky situations.

Lifestyle Computing Sector

In the Lifestyle Computing sector, Beauty Technologies will be available to interact with other devices in order to do things like making appointments, doing interactive performances, accessing data/media and sharing experiences [170]. Table 6.3 shows this sector's applications and its relation with Beauty Technology.

iSkin has another scenario of stickers with electronics embedded being created for acting as a smartwatch on the skin for controlling a smartphone [79]. NailO [173] embeds electronics on the fingernail for scrolling down pages in a computer and changing the color of a wearable by touching the nail's surface. NailDisplay [155] is a display mounted on a fingernail that controls a smartphone by zooming in and out the screen content. Tech Nails are used in AquaDJing, a under the water DJ controller; Twinkle Nails, an air piano [76].

Table 6.2 Communication sector

Applications	Functions	Products and prototypes
Personal interaction	Access voice, text email	iSkin [79], Hairware [99]
Group interaction	Social media communication	
Physical expression	Touch sensing	

Table 6.3 Lifestyle computing sector

Applications	Functions	Products
Use an organizer	Make appointments	iSkin [79], NailO
Data access	Notifications	[173], NailDisplay
Share experiences	Control smartphones	[155]

Sport and Fitness

The Sport and Fitness sector includes applications that promote and support sport and fitness activities such as fitness monitoring, outdoor navigation, activity tracking and sport performance [170]. For example, a sensor for detecting pulse rate and blood oxygen on flexible electronics are placed on the fingernail like a Band-Aid for fitness tracking such as during jogging and hiking [174]. Table 6.4 shows this sector's applications and its relation with Beauty Technology.

Wellness

The Wellness sector, differently than the Sport and Fitness sector, includes applications that are related to general wellbeing such as physiological monitoring, energy monitoring, emotion monitoring, eye care, posture correction and sleep monitoring [170]. Table 6.5 shows this sector's applications and its relation with Beauty Technology.

Winkymote [78] is an infrared remote controller for people with quadriplegic disabilities that triggers house appliances by blinking. Special effects makeup and sensors are placed on the user's face for sensing his voluntary muscles movements. Sunfriend [72] is a wristband that it is not directly attached to the skin but promotes skin's protection by giving feedback to the wearer whenever his UV exposure is excessive. Hairware [100] could also be used to detect stress when she constantly touches her hair.

Medical

The Medical sector includes applications that are required for professional medical use such as vital signs monitoring, chronic disease management and muscle movement monitoring. This sector differentiates from the previous one because special

Table 6.4 Sport and fitness sector

Applications	Functions	Products
Fitness monitoring, sport performance	Activity tracking	Band-aid for fitness [174]

Table 6.5 Wellness sector

Applications	Functions	Products
Body surface monitoring, sleep monitoring, posture correction	Devices for people with disabilities	Winkymote [78]
	Skin monitoring	Sunfriend [72]

Table 6.6 Medical sector

Applications	Functions	Products
Vital signs monitoring, disease management, movement monitoring	Measure disease changes	Google lens [175]
	Skin monitoring	MC10 cosmetics [127]

medical equipment regulations are required [170]. Table 6.6 shows this sector's applications and its relation with Beauty Technology.

Google Lens Project [175] is researching in miniaturize electronics in order to use contact lens for measuring levels of glucose. MC10 Cosmetics [127] is creating an electronic skin that could measure your skin moisture and provide skin care reports to improve user's skin health.

Security and Safety

The Security and Safety sector promotes the development of security and safety applications such as identity recognition, emergency services, environmental surveillance, rescue/tracking, military and other specialist professional uses. Table 6.7 shows this sector's applications and its relation with Beauty Technology.

Abrete Sesamo [76] unlocks a door when a secret combination of finger movements is read from RFID into nails. AERIALS [80] is an RFID in a shape of a tattoo that is attached to the skin for personal identification. Hairware [99] is used for sending messages in risky situations.

Table 6.7 Security and safety sector

Applications	Functions	Products
Identity recognition	Security profiling	Ábrete Sésamo [103], AERIALS [80]
Rescue / tracking environment	Help requests	Hairware [99]

Wearables, from their inception, were created for empowering the individual in different ways. We will like to conclude the book with three final statements that summarize this project motivation:

- We understand that the cyborg looks is not our future. We created unnoticeable wearable devices that not only camouflage the electronics within cosmetics, but also conceal interactions by using normal human behaviors as activators such as smiling, winking and touching one's hair.
- Our aim is to move from traditional to interactive cosmetics. We developed novel materials by intertwining cosmetics and electronics that may be ergonomically attached to the body surface i.e. skin, hair and fingernails.

- Beauty Technology may be applied to different contexts such as medical, arts, music and theatre; becoming a new subfield in Wearable Computing.

Annex 1
Awards

The following list shows the awards won by the Project Beauty Technology:

- *PRIX Ars Electronica 2015—Austria*
  [the next idea] voestalpine Art and Technology Grant
  Honourable Mention. Beauty Technology.
- *IUI 2015—USA.*
  First Prize. Best Demo. Project: Hairware
- *NUMA 2014—Finland*
  First Prize. Eighth annual international ubimedia competition, Beauty Tech.
- *HCII 2014—Greece*
  First Prize. Best paper: "FX e-makeup for Muscle Based Interaction."
- *TEI 2013—Spain*
  First Prize. Design Challenge. Project: Superheroes
- *ELA-ES 2013—Brazil*
  Third Prize. Category: PhD.
- *Mostra PUC 2013—Brazil*
  First Prize. PhD Project Prize: Innovations for a better life.
- *SBSC 2013—Brazil*
  Second Prize. Best paper: "Uma Abordagem Sistemática de Prototipação Colaborativa para a Criação de Tangíveis."

© Springer International Publishing Switzerland 2016
K. Vega, H. Fuks, *Beauty Technology*, Human–Computer Interaction Series,
DOI 10.1007/978-3-319-15762-7

Annex 2
Publications

The following list presents our publications related to Beauty Technology:

- [This Book] Beauty Technology: Designing seamless interfaces for Wearable Computing. (2015). Springer. Series: <u>Human–Computer Interaction Series</u>. Authors: Vega Katia, Fuks Hugo
- Vega, K., Cunha, M., Fuks, H.: Hairware: The conscious use of unconscious auto-contact behaviors. In: Proceedings of the 20th International Conference on Intelligent User Interfaces, IUI 2015, pp. 78–86. ACM, New York (2015)
- Vega, K., Cunha, M., Fuks, H.: Hairware: conductive hair extensions as a capacitive touch input device. In: Proceedings of the 20th International Conference on Intelligent User Interfaces Companion, IUI 2015. ACM, New York (2015)
- Vega, K., Aucelio, R., Fuks, H.: Hairware: designing seamless wearable devices. In: HCII (2015)
- Vega, K.: Beauty Technology as an Interactive Computing Platform. PhD Thesis. Advisor: Hugo Fuks (2014)
- Vega, K., Fuks, H.: Beauty technology: body surface computing. IEEE Computer **47**(4), 71–75 (2014)
- Vega, K., Fuks, H.: Beauty tech nails: interactive technology at your fingertips. In: Proceedings of the Eighth International Conference on Tangible, Embedded and Embodied Interaction, TEI 2014, pp. 61–64). ACM (2014)
- Vega, K., Arrieta, A., Esteves, F., Fuks, H.: FX e-makeup for muscle based interaction. In: Design, User Experience, and Usability. User Experience Design for Everyday Life Applications and Services, HCII 2014, pp. 643–652. Springer, Berlin (2014)
- Vega, K., Fuks, H.: Beauty technology as an interactive computing platform. In: Proceedings of the 2013 ACM International Conference on Interactive Tabletops and Surfaces, ITS 2013, pp. 357–360. ACM (2013)
- Vega, K., Fuks, H.: Beauty technology: muscle based computing interaction. In: Proceedings of the 2013 ACM International Conference on Interactive Tabletops and Surfaces, ITS 2013, pp. 469–474. ACM (2013)

© Springer International Publishing Switzerland 2016   79
K. Vega, H. Fuks, *Beauty Technology*, Human–Computer Interaction Series,
DOI 10.1007/978-3-319-15762-7

- Cardador, D., Ugulino, W., Vega, K., Filippo, D., Raposo, A., Fuks, H.: Uma Abordagem Sistemática de Prototipação Colaborativa para a Criação de Tangíveis. In: Proceedings of the X Brazilian Symposium in Collaborative Systems, p. 56 (2013)
- Vega, K.F.C., Flanagan, P.J., Fuks, H.: Blinklifier: a case study for prototyping wearable computers in technology and visual arts. In: Design, User Experience, and Usability. User Experience in Novel Technological Environments HCII 2013, pp. 439–445. Springer, Heidelberg (2013)
- Flanagan, P.J., Vega, K.F.C.: Future fashion–at the interface. In: Design, User Experience, and Usability. Design Philosophy, Methods, and Tools. HCII 2013, pp. 48–57. Springer, Heidelberg (2013)
- Vega, K.F.C., Fuks, H.: Empowering electronic divas through beauty technology. In: Design, User Experience, and Usability. User Experience in Novel Technological Environments, HCII 2013, pp. 237–245. Springer (2013)
- Flanagan, P.J., Vega, K., Fuks, H.: Blinklifier: the power of feedback loops for amplifying expressions through bodily worn objects. In: Proceedings of APCHI, pp. 641–642 (2012)

Annex 3
Exhibitions and Demos

Beauty Technology prototypes were exhibited in different conferences and fairs. The following list presents the exhibitions and demonstrations related to Beauty Technology.

- Brazilian Computer Society –SBC (Brazil, 2015). SEMISH. Presentation: "From Traditional to Interactive Cosmetics"
- Maker Faire Shenzhen (China, 2015). Presentation: "Hack your Body with Cosmetics"
- I Encontro de Projetos em Ambientes Interativos (Brazil, 2015). Presentation: Beauty Technology
- Make it Wearables (USA, 2014). Intel. Project: AquaDJing
- Makers in Brazil: Wearables & IoT (Brazil, 2014). Wearable Wednesday. Presentation: Beauty Technology, Transformando o Corpo numa Plataforma de Interação
- Cuerpo Digital (Mexico, 2014). Wear+D. Project: AquaDJing, Beauty Technology presentation
- Digital Revolution at the Barbican Center (UK, 2014), National Museum of Science and Technology (Sweden, 2014). Project: Kinisi
- Make Fashion (Canada, 2014). Project: Blinklifier
- Demo and paper presentation: TEI'14, 8th International Conference on Tangible, Embedded and Embodied Interaction. Demo Session (Germany, 2014). Project: AquaDJing, Twinkle Nails
- Session Chair and paper presentation: HCII'14, 15th International Conference on Human-Computer Interaction (Greece, 2014). Session: "Novel Wearable Interfaces: Beauty Technology"
- BITS (Brazil, 2014). Presentation: Beauty Technology
- Semana Ciencia e Tecnologia, Unirio. (Brazil, 2014). Presentation: Beauty Technology
- Wearable Futures (UK, 2013). Project Twinkle Nails
- Women 2.0. Fashion Show (USA, 2013). Projects: AquaDJing, Superhero

K. Vega, H. Fuks, *Beauty Technology*, Human–Computer Interaction Series, DOI 10.1007/978-3-319-15762-7

- UIST'13, 26th ACM Symposium on User Interface Software and Technology. Student Contest (Scotland, 2013). Project: AquaDJing
- Maker Faire Bay Area (USA, 2013). Projects: Superhero, Twinkle Nails
- Mostra PUC (Brazil, 2013). Project: Twinkle Nails
- TEI'13, 7th International Conference on Tangible, Embedded and Embodied Interaction. Design Challenge (Spain, 2013). Project: Superhero
- Conversatorio Fundación Telefónica. Arte y Estética en Wearable Computers (Peru, 2013). Projects: Arcana, Gimmickiano, AquaDJing
- Sydney VIVID festival. Haptic Interface Pop-Up exhibition (Australia, 2013). Project Blinklifier
- Asian Premiere of Multimedia Art: New York Paris Hong Kong Change your Perception (Hong Kong, 2013). Project Blinklifier.
- JMGA 15th Biennial Conference Participation + Exchange. Participate Exhibition. (Australia, 2012). Project Blinklifier
- Haptic Interface Exhibition (Hong Kong, 2012). Project Blinklifier
- Beyond Wearable (China, 2012). Project Blinklifier

Annex 4
Media Coverage

Beauty Technology attracted the following press coverage. The list contains several press releases talking about this technology.

Ifanr

位科学家告诉我们, 如何让科技变美?
http://www.ifanr.com/535457
Mon, 29 Jun 2015
你可曾想过, 女生用以装饰的假睫毛和指甲贴, 会启发到一位科学家去打破科技与美丽的界线, 将这两个一直以来相关性不大的领域结合在一起, 并最终发明出了之前只有科幻电影里才有的产品?
位科学家就是来自秘鲁的 Katia Vega, 她通过赋予化妆各种技术元素, 让女生在装扮自己的过程中也能体验到科技的强大。

Wearables Technologies

Technology in disguise! Wearable Technologies for Cosmetics.
http://www.wearable-technologies.com/2015/06/technology-in-disguise-wearable-technologies-for-cosmetics/
Sat, 1 June 2015
Katia Vega calls herself a designer of Beauty Technology. In the past she has created make-up to act like a switch for LED lights, and fingernails to radio actively control sound waves. Her teams newest creation to the wearable realm is call Hairware: the conscious use of unconscious auto-contact behaviors. This product alters the normally stylistic use of hair extensions into a seamless form of digital communication…

© Springer International Publishing Switzerland 2016
K. Vega, H. Fuks, *Beauty Technology*, Human–Computer Interaction Series,
DOI 10.1007/978-3-319-15762-7

PSFK

Hair Extensions Let You Text Without Interrupting Your Conversation
http://www.psfk.com/2015/06/smart-extensions-send-text-messages-hairware.html
Sat, 1 June 2015
The wearable technology trend knows no bounds with the concept now coming to
the fore within the beauty sector. A new brand named Hairware, with the tagline,
"The conscious use of unconscious auto-contact behaviors," is now translating
hair-related gestures into modern-day messaging techniques.

O Globo

O poder do charme
http://g1.globo.com/jornal-nacional/noticia/2015/05/pesquisadora-mostra-que-
mexidas-no-cabelo-podem-comandar-celular.html
Fri, 8 May 2015
Cabelo também se transforma em uma ferramenta de proteção para as mulheres:
sem chamar a atenção, elas podem enviar mensagens de socorro.

Adrafruit

Internet of Hair
https://blog.adafruit.com/2015/04/15/internet-of-hair-wearablewednesday
Wed, 14 Apr 2015
Katia Vega has already worked with eyelashes and conductive makeup to trigger
drones. Now she is taking things undercover with touch sensitive hair extensions, according to Bits & Pieces from the Embedded Design World. Sounds
weird, but it's great if you want to control something without bringing attention
to the action—just touch your hair.

Heise

Hairware: Eine Haarverlängerung zur Steuerung des Smartphones
http://www.heise.de/newsticker/meldung/Hairware-Eine-Haarverlaengerung-zur-
Steuerung-des-Smartphones-2602017.html
Mon, 13 Apr 2015
Das unverfängliche Streichen durch die Haare könnte in Zukunft, vom Gegenüber
unbemerkt, Aktionen auf dem eigenen Smartphone auslösen. Das schlägt
zumindest ein Unternehmen aus Brasilien vor.

CNET

<u>Clandestinely control your smartphone by stroking your hair</u>
http://www.cnet.com/news/clandestinely-control-your-smartphone-by-stroking-
    your-hair/
Sun, 12 Apr 2015
The feeling of being stuck in a threatening situation is one known to many women—
    and sometimes, reaching for an emergency help app—such as Circle of 6—could
    potentially cause more danger. But what if there was a means whereby a natural
    gesture could trigger an app without alerting anyone nearby?

Fashioning Tech

<u>Hairware—Interactive Hair Extensions Augment Natural Gestures</u>
http://fashioningtech.com/profiles/blogs/hairware-interactive-hair-extensions-aug-
    ment-natural-gestures
Sun, 12 Apr 2015
She's done it again: Beauty technologist, Katia Vega (together with fellow research-
    ers, Marcio Cunha and Hugo Fuks) is once more pushing the boundaries of wear-
    able electronics with her latest project, Hairware.

Techxplore

<u>Hair today, communication trigger tomorrow</u>
http://techxplore.com/news/2015-04-hair-today-trigger-tomorrow.html
Sat, 11 Apr 2015
Beauty technology? Don't be concerned if at first you missed the mark. "Beauty
    technology" does not refer to how ingredients are processed and packaged on
    shampoo and soap assembly lines. Katia Vega is a post-doc researcher with a
    PhD in computer science from the Pontifical Catholic University of Rio de
    Janeiro; she can demonstrate what it is. She has been working on wearables and
    the virtual world, bringing beauty technology to a different place in technology.

Mind Press

<u>Donne addio tastiera: Con Hairware gli sms si inviano accarezzando i capelli</u>
http://tech.mindpress.it/5528/donne-addio-tastiera-con-hairware-si-inviano-sms-
    accarezzando-capelli/
Sat, 11 Apr 2015

Sembra irreale, ma grazie ad Hairware mandare sms giocherellando con una ciocca di capelli è possibile, ed è solo una delle tante funzioni del sistema che trasforma l'auto-contatto in controllo a distanza.

Alfa

Nuo šiol moterys gali pasijusti kaip slaptosios agentės
http://www.alfa.lt/straipsnis/49831392/nuo-siol-moterys-gali-pasijusti-kaip-slapto-sios-agentes
Fri, 10 Apr 2015
Gal tai skamba ir neįtikėtinai, tačiau specialistai sukūrė technologiją, kuri leidžia slapta valdyti savo išmanųjį telefoną ar planšetinį kompiuterį. Technologija "Hairware" buvo sukurta vadovaujant mokslininkei Katiai Vegai iš Katalikų popiežiaus universiteto Rio de Žaneire, rašo Newscientist.com

Thanhnien

Xoắn tóc để điều khiển smartphone
http://www.thanhnien.com.vn/cong-nghe-thong-tin/xoan-toc-de-dieu-khien--smartphone-550597.html
Sat, 11 Apr 2015
(TNO) Lần sau, nếu bạn trò chuyện với một cô gái có vẻ như luôn lơ đãng nghịch tóc, có thể là đối phương đang có ý định khác ngoài chuyện làm duyên làm dáng.

Pshy.org

Hair today, communication trigger tomorrow
http://phys.org/news/2015-04-hair-today-trigger-tomorrow.html
Sat, 11 Apr 2015
Beauty technology? Don't be concerned if at first you missed the mark. "Beauty technology" does not refer to how ingredients are processed and packaged on shampoo and soap assembly lines. Katia Vega is a post-doc researcher with a PhD in computer science from the Pontifical Catholic University of Rio de Janeiro; she can demonstrate what it is. She has been working on wearables and the virtual world, bringing beauty technology to a different place in technology.

Discovery

Touching Your Hair Controls Your Smartphone
http://news.discovery.com/tech/gear-and-gadgets/touching-your-hair-controls-
   your-smartphone-150410.htm
Fri, 10 Apr 2015
The next time you have a conversation with someone who seems to be innocently
   playing with her hair, you might want to think twice about her intentions.
A new technology called Hairware, invented by Katia Vega of the Pontifical
   Catholic University of Rio de Janeiro, Brazil, allows people to control their
   smartphones by activating sensors hidden in their hair.

Gizmodo

Con esta tecnología basta tocarse el pelo para usar el móvil en secreto
http://es.gizmodo.com/con-esta-tecnologia-basta-tocarse-el-pelo-para-usar-
   el-1696768786
Thu, 9 Apr 2015
Ni relojes, ni pulseras, ni anillos, el próximo mando para interactuar con el smartphone
   podríamos llevarlo en nuestra propia cabeza y nadie se daría cuenta. El invento se
   llama Hairware, y se trata de extensiones de cabello indistinguibles de nuestro
   propio pelo que activan diferentes funciones con solo tocar el mechón correcto.

Digital Trends

Like something out of a James Bond flick, these hair extensions can remotely control electronic devices
http://www.digitaltrends.com/cool-tech/hairware-smart-hair-extensions/
Thu, 9 Apr 2015
In news that seems like it was plucked straight out of a James Bond flick, a Brazilian
   inventor has developed an innovative new wearable gadget that allows users to
   discreetly control electronic devices by stroking their hair.

Terra

Hairware: controla tu smartphone con tu cabellera
http://noticias.terra.es/tecnologia/hairware-controla-tu-smartphone-con-tu-cabeller
   a,38a34c73710ac410VgnVCM4000009bcceb0aRCRD.html
Thu, 9 Apr 2015
El término "smarthair" podría no decirte nada, pero cuando conocimos Hairware,
   fue el primer término que se nos vino a la cabeza.

New Scientist

Control Smartphones with a stroke of your hair
https://www.newscientist.com/article/dn27312-control-smartphones-with-a-stroke-
of-your-hair
Thu, 9 Apr 2015
Is that woman absent-mindedly stroking her hair? Or is she actually recording a
conman's deception and broadcasting his location? It sounds unlikely—but
that's just one possible application of a system that lets you turn your hair into a
covert trigger for your apps.

Make Magazine

Wearables Special Edition
http://makezine.com/magazine/make-43/jellyfish-dress-mood-sweater-and-
8-more-insanely-cool-light-up-wearables/
Tue, 27 Jan 2015
Could your expressions act as an interface? A wink, a smile, or a raised eyebrow
triggers sensors attached to various muscles and relays the information to a
microcontroller that sets off different light patterns in LEDs attached to the face
and hair.

Daily Collegian

The science of beauty shows the future of cosmetics
http://dailycollegian.com/2014/11/03/the-science-of-beauty-shows-the-future-of-
cosmetics/
Mon, 3 Nov 2014
Meanwhile, Katia Vega, a computer scientist, has developed eyelashes and press-on
nails with multiple functions. Demonstrated last year at the Interactive Tabletops
and Surfaces conference at the University of St. Andrews, U.K., models wore
fake eyelashes that could control drones by blinking, and press-on nails acted as
a miniature Theremin by playing an air piano or D.J.-ing a tub of water.

Techli

11 Coolest Wearable Tech Pieces of the Past Year
http://techli.com/2014/12/11-coolest-wearable-tech-pieces-of-the-past-year/#

Fri, 19 Dec 2014

What's the coolest wearable technology to debut in 2014 and why do you think it's a game changer?

The following answers are provided by members of Young Entrepreneur Council (YEC), an invite-only organization comprised of the world's most promising young entrepreneurs. In partnership with Citi, YEC recently launched StartupCollective, a free virtual mentorship program that helps millions of entrepreneurs start and grow businesses.

Atmel

Rewind: 25 wow-worthy wearables from 2014

http://blog.atmel.com/2014/12/10/rewind-25-must-know-wearables-from-2014/

Thu, 11 Dec 2014

As we turn the page on 2014, we're taking a quick look back at some of our favorite wearables from the last 12 months. While analysts predict the market to experience an uptick heading into 2015, we can only wait and see what new products emerge!

O Globo

Tecnologias vestíveis: mercado em ascensão no Brasil e no mundo

http://oglobo.globo.com/economia/emprego/tecnologias-vestiveis-mercado-em-ascensao-no-brasil-no-mundo-13619252

Sun, 17 Ago 2014

O futuro como imaginado no desenho animado "Os Jetsons" está cada vez mais próximo—e abre mercado para quem quer investir em novidades. As tecnologias vestíveis—wearables, em inglês—de mansinho começam a chegar ao Brasil, não só de fora, mas também de dentro do país.

Intel

Intuitive, Wearable Gesture Control is the Wave of Future Tech

http://iq.intel.com/intuitive-gesture-control-is-wave-of-future-wearable-tech/

Tue, 1 Apr 2014

In The Future of Wearable Tech, iQ by Intel and PSFK Labs explore the evolving form and function of our Internet-connected devices. This series, based on a recent report, looks at the rise of wearable technologies and their impact on consumer lifestyles.

The Creators Project

Make It Wearable Part 3: Human Expression
http://thecreatorsproject.vice.com/blog/make-it-wearable-part-3-human-expression
Thu, 6 Mar 2014
Katia Vega has been on The Creators Project's radar for a while, as she makes
   accessories and cosmetics that are both beautiful and insanely futuristic. Whether
   it's her makeup that controls drones, or eyelashes that can control the lights in a
   room—she's blowing our minds while enhancing our personal features.

CNET

Científica peruana quiere hacer de tu cara una interfaz
http://www.cnet.com/es/noticias/cientifica-peruana-quiere-hacer-tu-cara-una-
   interfaz/
Wed, 12 Feb 2014
Tras crear una línea de "tecnología de la belleza," Katia Vega desarrolla una línea
   para usar los músculos de la cara para controlar dispositivos.

Fast Company

These Fake Eyelashes Can Control Your TV
http://www.fastcoexist.com/3025541/these-fake-eyelashes-can-control-your-tv
Thru, 06 Feb 2014
Wearable tech as makeup could help quadriplegics control their environments with
   the wink of an eye.

Wired UK

Superhero remote control eyelashes: the wearable tech we can get onboard with
http://www.wired.co.uk/news/archive/2014-01-28/motion-control-makeup
Tue, 28 Jan 2014
When 33-year-old quadriplegic Felipe Esteves saw Katia Vega levitate a small
   drone just by blinking at it, he knew that was the kind of superhero he wanted to
   be. Wearing a white wig to keep her secret identity intact, channeling X-Men's
   Storm, Vega was demonstrating her superhero tech at an expo. Each time she
   blinked with purpose, a tiny circuit nearly invisible to onlookers completed and

instructed a controller to move the drone. That circuit was hidden under her wig, and was completed every time a pair of metallic false eyelashes met for a long enough time and connected to conductive eyeliner Vega was wearing. Signals were transmitted to a Zigbee radio, with the receiver kept in the superhero's handbag. Sometimes, her blinks instructed animated images that read "POW, Bam, Zap" to pop up.

PSFK

Makeup with embedded electronics helps the disabled control their devices
http://www.psfk.com/2014/01/embedded-electronic-makeup.html
Fri, 24 Jan 2014
Advancements in wearable technology enable people with disabilities to carry on with normal daily functions.

Cisco

Startup trends for 2014
http://newsroom.cisco.com/feature-content?type=webcontent&articleId=1308686
Mon, 13 Jan 2014
A look at the wearable, shareable & social trends you'll see in the coming year.

PSFK

The Future of Wearable Tech. Key trends driven the Form and Function of Personal Devices
http://www.psfk.com/publishing/future-of-wearable-tech
Wed, 8 Jan 2014
This report examines ten key trends that are impacting the future of wearable technologies with a focus on the basic features, form and functions of these devices and technologies and what they might replace. Aided by the increased processing speed of chips, capacity of batteries and precision of sensor technologies, devices are becoming smaller, faster and more feature heavy, nearly replacing entire electronic categories in the process and furthermore impacting the way we live, work and socialize. As we plan for the future, PSFK Labs in collaboration with iQ by Intel is excited for the opportunity to contribute its point of view to this ongoing conversation.

Mashable

Smart Eyelashes and Fingernails: The Next Wave of Wearable Tech
http://mashable.com/2013/12/21/programmable-makeup/
Sat, 21 Dec 2013
It was crowded on the sidewalks in Hong Kong. Early morning commuters, shoulders tightly pressed against the strangers walking next to them, moved in a sluggish blob through each brimming intersection. Katia Vega didn't mind the congestion. If anything, it made for ideal people-watching.

Women 2.0

Katia Vega to Showcase Aqua DJ Set and Drone That Reacts to Body Movement
http://women2.com/katia-vega-showcase-aqua-dj-set-drone-reacts-body-movement/#G2p5hfVrbfEoDQwd.99
Tue, 12 Nov 2013
Our newest fashion show addition is pushing the boundaries of wearable tech. Learn what she will be showcasing at our conference.

Fashioning Tech

It's All in a Wink
http://www.fashioningtech.com/profiles/blogs/it-s-all-in-a-wink-1
Thru, 31 Oct 2013
Katia Vega is a Beauty Tech Designer and is currently a PhD candidate in Computer Science at the Department of Informatics from the Pontifical Catholic University of Rio de Janeiro (Brazil) under the supervision of Prof. Hugo Fuks. She describes beauty technology as an emergent field in wearable computer using software in innovative ways.

Nextmedia

戴假睫毛通電　眨眼開燈
http://hk.apple.nextmedia.com/international/art/20131026/18479867
Sat, 26 Oct 2013
眨一眨眼可為電子裝置供電開啟燈泡、手指頭一動即可打開上鎖的門戶，
不必成為特務都可擁有這些「特異功能」。巴西科學家維加 (Katia Vega)
將眼影、假眼睫毛和指甲加入無線電裝置,令美容與科技合二為一。

The Creators Project

Viral Style: Makeup That Drives Drones And A Bra That Tweets
http://thecreatorsproject.vice.com/blog/viral-style-drones
Fri, 25 Oct 2013
A weekly roundup of what's happening at the intersection of tech and fashion.
Drone-controlling beauty tech of the week.

Golem

Elektronische Wimpern lassen Dioden leuchten
http://www.golem.de/news/blinklifier-elektronische-wimpern-lassen-dioden--
    leuchten-1310-102231.html
Fri, 18 Oct 2013
Blinklifier ist ein neuartiges Eingabegerät, das mit den Augen gesteuert wird: Es
    erkennt ein Augenzwinkern und löst eine Aktion aus. Gleichzeitig soll es die
    Träger verschönern.

Imena

Электронный макияж позволит управлять мобильными устройствами
http://www.imena.ua/blog/elektro-makiyazh
Fri, 18 Oct 2013
Американский инженер Катя Вега (Katia Vega) сообщила о создании
    "электронного макияжа," состоящего из микроэлементов, которые
    располагаются на глазных веках.

CNet

Electronic makeup lets you control gadgets with a wink
http://news.cnet.com/8301-17938_105-57607997-1/electronic-makeup-lets-you-
    control-gadgets-with-a-wink/
Fri, 18 Oct 2013
Fingernails embedded with RFID tags? Computer scientist Katia Vega creates
    Beauty Technology, a range of cosmetics and accessories that conduct electricity
    and control devices.

The Times

Metallic make-up that turns on lights
http://www.thetimes.co.uk/tto/technology/article3897627.ece?CMP=OTH-
    gnws-standard-2013_10_17
Fri, 18 Oct 2013
The hi-tech cosmetics were unveiled at an Interactive and Surface conference at the
    University of St Andrews

IEEE

Computer scientist Katia Vega has developed a set of conducting cosmetics that can
    be applied to your fingernails or eyelashes to control technology
https://www.facebook.com/photo.php?fbid=573082502746389&set=a.176108879
    110422.62121.176104589110851&type=1&theater
Fri, 18 Oct 2013
Computer scientist Katia Vega has developed a set of conducting cosmetics that can
    be applied to your fingernails or eyelashes to control technology.

PSFK

Electronic Eyelashes control mobile devices with a wink
http://www.psfk.com/2013/10/electronic-eyelashes-control-devices.html
Thu, 17 Oct 2013
Beauty tech designer Katia Vega developed cosmetics that can activate various
    equipment

Popsci

A Tiny Helicopter Controlled With A Wink
http://www.popsci.com/article/gadgets/watch-tiny-helicopter-controlled-wink
Thu, 17 Oct 2013
Special metallic makeup could put the face back into "user interface."

Mnn

Electronic make-up lets you control the lights with a wink
http://www.mnn.com/lifestyle/natural-beauty-fashion/stories/electronic-make-up-
    lets-you-control-the-lights-with-a-wink

Thu, 17 Oct 2013

Now you can look electric and, well, actually be electric too. Researchers have
developed electronic makeup that turns your face into a remote control.

Thomas net

Light Friday: Eight Mental Illnesses Caused by the Internet
http://news.thomasnet.com/IMT/2013/10/18/light-friday-8-mental-
illnesses-caused-by-the-internet/
Thu, 17 Oct 2013

Wearable Beauty Technology Lights up a Room One engineer has found a way to
infuse beauty with technology to create conducting cosmetics that are capable of
activating electronics and levitating objects. Katia Vega, the makeup tech mas-
termind, is currently a Ph.D. candidate in computer science at Pontifical Catholic
University of Rio de Janeiro in Brazil and has developed chemically metalized
eyelashes, RFID nails, and makeup that "connect sensors, actuators and their
connections in an attractive way that the wearer's observers would not notice the
hidden circuit," Vega notes on her website.

New Scientist

Metallic make-up lets you launch drones with a wink
http://www.newscientist.com/article/dn24412-metallic-makeup-lets-you-launch-
drones-with-a-wink.html#.UmVcDBAwdpd
Wed, 16 Oct 2013

When Katia Vega winks, strange things happen: a miniature drone takes to the air,
or a hundred LEDs in her hair sparkle like a Christmas tree. It works because she
has developed a range of conducting cosmetics that let her activate electronics
with a flip of her eyelids

Boing Boing

Conductive cosmetics to control mobile devices
http://boingboing.net/2013/10/16/conductive-cosmetics-to-contro.html
Wed, 16 Oct 2013

Computer scientist Katia Vega has developed conductive eye shadow and false eyelashes that can be used to control wearable computers. For example, an extended
blink could trigger your phone's camera.

Fast Company

This Makeup Lets You Launch Drones With Just A Blink Of An Eye
http://www.fastcompany.com/3020130/fast-feed/this-makeup-lets-you-launch-
    drones-with-just-a-blink-of-an-eye
Wed, 16 Oct 2013
Brazilian scientist Katia Vega has developed cosmetics with the ability to launch a
    drone or open a door.

Future Tech Report

Using cosmetics to control gadgets
http://futuretechreport.com/post/64679126997/using-cosmetics-to-control-
    gadgets-one-of-the
Mon, 21 Oct 2013
One of the most intriguing developments to come out of the recent ACM Interactive
    Tabletops and Surfaces Conference is new work from the Brazilian scientist,
    Katia Vega, who offered up something called "electro-cosmetics," or the field of
    research into controlling electronics using cosmetic make-up.

Refinery 29

This Is NOT Science Fiction: A Woman Can Control Drones With Her …
http://www.refinery29.com/2013/10/55603/metallic-makeup-controls-drones
Fri, 18 Oct 2013
We can do a lot with our makeup: change our look, highlight a certain feature,
    attract attention…the list goes on. What our list doesn't include, though, is the
    ability to, um, control drones. That's apparently simply because we're not Katia
    Vega, a computer scientist who has developed makeup that can literally activate
    electronics. Wait, what?

Gizmodo

Electronic Make-Up Lets You Activate Gadgets By Blinking
http://gizmodo.com/electronic-make-up-lets-you-activate-gadgets-by-
    blinkin-1446288892
Thu, 17 Oct 2013
Ever wanted to a launch a fleet of killer drones with the blink of an eye? Good news,
    researchers have just the thing.

Stuff Tv

Fully Charged: Enter the Matrix, Android PCs, and how to scramble …
http://www.stuff.tv/gopro/fully-charged-fire-eating-how-scramble-drone-blink-
eye-and/news
Wed, 16 Oct 2013
Ever wanted to a launch a fleet of killer drones with the blink of an eye? Good news,
researchers have just the thing.

Ubergizmo

Makeup Gets Conductive
http://www.ubergizmo.com/2013/10/makeup-gets-conductive/
Fri, 18 Oct 2013
Putting on makeup might not be the same any more in the future, as wearable technology takes on a whole new level of interactivity. With the clever application of
conductive makeup in common beauty items such as false eyelashes, nails and
eyeshadow, computer scientist Katia Vega managed to figure out a way to make
conductive elements as well as sensors part of transforming an ordinary makeup
into gadget-activating remote controls.

Apparata

Elektronische make-up bestuurt gadgets met een knipoog
http://www.apparata.nl/nieuws/elektronische-make-up-bestuurt-gadgets-met-
een-knipoog-3788
Wed, 16 Oct 2013
Dus je wilt je gadgets op afstand bedienen, maar bent te lui om de afstandsbediening
te pakken en Google Glass kan je niet betalen. Gelukkig heeft je vrouw/vriendin
een dikke laag make-up op en kan zo van kanaal wisselen. Wait, what?

O Globo

Conheça sete criações inovadoras que saíram de universidades
http://oglobo.globo.com/educacao/conheca-sete-criacoes-inovadoras-que-sairam-
de-universidades-9632117#ixzz2iNPCMgPI
Wed, 23 Oct 2013
A aluna do curso de doutorado do Departamento de Informática da PUC-Rio, Katia
Vega, desenvolve pesquisas sobre o conceito de "Beauty Technology," que
agrega tecnologia a diferentes partes do corpo humano. A pesquisadora já

desenvolveu cílios postiços capazes de emitir comandos eletrônicos através do movimento do piscar dos olhos, como passar slides em uma apresentação, e criou unhas postiças com dispositivos que emitem comandos como acender luzes e abrir portas.

O Globo

Feira com trabalhos tecnológicos da PUC-Rio deve atrair 75 mil visitantes
http://g1.globo.com/globo-news/jornal-das-dez/videos/t/todos-os-videos/v/
    feira-com-trabalhos-tecnologicos-da-puc-rio-deve-atrair-75-mil--
    visitantes/2761613/
Wed, 23 Oct 2013
São trabalhos de alta tecnologia, muitos deles com iniciativas sustentáveis. Os projetos, protótipos e até produtos criados pelos alunos, será exibidos durante quatro dias na universidade.

Tech tudo

Pesquisadora cria sistema que controla objetos pelo movimento de olhos e dedos
http://www.techtudo.com.br/noticias/noticia/2013/07/pesquisadora-cria-sistema-
    que-controla-objetos-pelo-movimento-de-olhos-e-dedos.html
Mon, 8 Jul 2013
Ao menos uma vez na vida você quis poder controlar um objeto com um piscar de olhos, não é? Saiba que essa realidade está cada vez mais próxima. Uma pesquisa resultou na criação de cílios postiços e unhas de acrigel, capazes de controlar apresentações de slides, equipamentos de DJ, iluminação e uma infinidade de objetos. O estudo, desenvolvido na PUC-Rio, é feito pela peruana Kátia Vega, com supervisão do professor Hugo Fuks.

CNN

Bionic fashion: Wearable tech that will turn man into machine by 2015
http://edition.cnn.com/2013/07/25/tech/innovation/bionic-fashion-wearable-
    tech-2015/index.html
Mon, 5 Aug 2013
The field of wearable technology is rich with exploration of human emotion—and headwear that would turn Padmé Amidala green with envy. The flirty Blinklifier is a concept by Tricia Flanagan and Katia Vega. It's fitted with LEDs that respond to specific eye-movement and could take flirting to a new level. Researchers hope the result will give people more visual clues about how their friends are feeling.

Editora Abril

Google Glass—Por que ter um computador no corpo
http://info.abril.com.br/revista/extras/index.shtml?ed=330
Mon, 1 Jul 2013
Conectado à internet, o Google Glass é pioneiro de uma tendência que deve nos
  levar à computação de vestir

Sensoree

Move over Google Glass, we have Beauty Technology
http://sensoree.com/move-over-google-glass-we-have-beauty-technology/
Fri, 24 May 2013
Conductive make-up, magnetic finger nails, a blink controller that levitates objects
  with blinking? Take off my Google Glass and paint it on me!

O Globo

Aluna da PUC-Rio cria cílios que controlam objetos ao piscar
http://g1.globo.com/tecnologia/noticia/2013/04/aluna-da-puc-rio-cria-cilios-que-
  controlam-objetos-ao-piscar.html
Wed, 17 Apr 2013
Katia Vega recebeu o prêmio TEI Design Challenge, em Barcelona. Cílios usam
  tecnologia conhecida como "computação vestível."
Katia, que mora no Rio de Janeiro desde 2008, metalizou os cílios postiços com
  prata e outros elementos químicos para que eles parecessem pretos e naturais.
  Com o controle remoto de um pequeno orbitador escondido no bolso, Katia
  podia ativá-lo apenas ao piscar os olhos.

References

1. Starner, T.E.: Wearable computing and contextual awareness, pp. 23–25. Doctoral Dissertation, Massachusetts Institute of Technology, Cambridge, MA (1999)
2. Hooke, R.: Micrographia: Or Some Physiological Descriptions of Minute Bodies Made by Magnifying Glasses: With Observations and Inquiries Thereupon. By R. Hooke, Fellow of the Royal Society. John Martyn, printer to the Royal Society, and are to be sold at his shop at the Bell a little without Temple Barr (1966).
3. Mann, S.: Humanistic computing: "WearComp" as a new framework and application for intelligent signal processing. Proc. IEEE **86**, 2123–2151 (1998)
4. Ranck, J.: The wearable computing market: a global analysis (2012)
5. Pearson, I.: The future of fashion. J. Commun. Netw. **4**, 68 (2005)
6. Wagner, S., Bonderover, E., Jordan, W.B., Sturm, J.C.: Electrotextiles: concepts and challenges. Int. J. High Speed Electron. Syst. **12**, 391–399 (2002)
7. Buechley, L., Eisenberg, M.: Fabric PCBs, electronic sequins, and socket buttons: techniques for e-textile craft. Pers. Ubiquit. Comput. **13**, 133–150 (2009)
8. Berzowska, J.: Electronic textiles: wearable computers, reactive fashion, and soft computation. Textile J. Cloth Cult. **3**, 58–75 (2005)
9. Buechley, L., Eisenberg, M., Catchen, J., Crockett, A.: The LilyPad Arduino: using computational textiles to investigate engagement, aesthetics, and diversity in computer science education. In: Proceedings of the SIGCHI Conference on Human Factors in Computing Systems, pp. 423–432 (2008)
10. Toeters, M., Jacobs, R., Hoitink, A., Grant, M.: Solar fiber. http://www.solarfiber.nl/en/
11. Pushparaj, V.L., Shaijumon, M.M., Kumar, A., Murugesan, S., Ci, L., Vajtai, R., Linhardt, R.J., Nalamasu, O., Ajayan, P.M.: Flexible energy storage devices based on nanocomposite paper. Proc. Natl. Acad. Sci. **104**, 13574–13577 (2007)
12. Shenck, N.S., Paradiso, J.A.: Energy scavenging with shoe-mounted piezoelectrics. IEEE Micro **21**, 30–42 (2001)
13. Kizhner, N.: Energy addicts. http://www.naomikizhner.com/#!final-project--energy-addicts/c7q0
14. Kim, D.-H., Lu, N., Ma, R., Kim, Y.-S., Kim, R.-H., Wang, S., Wu, J., Won, S.M., Tao, H., Islam, A., et al.: Epidermal electronics. Science **333**, 838–843 (2011)
15. Takei, K.: Human interactive wearable devices: applications of artificial electronic skins and smart bandages. In: Design, User Experience, and Usability. User Experience Design for Everyday Life Applications and Services, pp. 710–718. Springer (2014)
16. Google: Google glass. http://www.google.com.br/glass/start/
17. Peeble: Pebble: E-paper watch for iPhone and android. https://getpebble.com

© Springer International Publishing Switzerland 2016
K. Vega, H. Fuks, *Beauty Technology*, Human–Computer Interaction Series,
DOI 10.1007/978-3-319-15762-7

18. Adafruit: Wearables. http://www.adafruit.com/blog/category/wearables/
19. Seeedstudio: Wearables. http://www.seeedstudio.com/depot/category_products?themes_id=1419
20. Sparkfun: Wearables. https://www.sparkfun.com/categories/204
21. Intel: This tiny brain for wearables is cute as a button. http://iq.intel.com/tiny-brain-wearables-cute-button/
22. McRae, L., Hess, B.: LucyandBart. http://www.lucymcrae.net
23. Park, S.: LED eyelashes (2009)
24. Seymour, S.: Functional Aesthetics. Springer, Vienna (2010)
25. Wikipedia: History of cosmetics. https://en.wikipedia.org/wiki/History_of_cosmetics
26. Amos, J.: Ancient "paint factory" unerthed. http://www.bbc.com/news/science-environment-15257259
27. Chaudhri, S.K., Jain, N.K., et al.: History of cosmetics. Asian J. Pharm. **3**, 164 (2009)
28. Cosmeticsinfo.org: A history of cosmetics from ancient times. http://www.cosmeticsinfo.org/Ancient-history-cosmetics
29. Tapsoba, I., Arbault, S., Walter, P., Amatore, C.: Finding out Egyptian Gods' secret using analytical chemistry: biomedical properties of Egyptian black makeup revealed by amperometry at single cells. Anal. Chem. **82**, 457–460 (2009)
30. Parish, L.C., Crissey, J.T.: Cosmetics: a historical review. Clin. Dermatol. **6**, 1–4 (1988)
31. Diamandopoulos, A., Kolonas, L., Grapsa-Kotrotsou, M.: Use of lead cosmetics in Bronze-Age Greece. Lancet **344**, 754–755 (1994)
32. Forslind, B., Lindberg, M.: Skin, Hair, and Nails: Structure and Function. CRC Press, Boca Raton (2003)
33. historyofcosmetics.net: Cosmetics history and facts
34. Organovo: L'Oreal USA announces research partnership with organovo to develop 3-d bioprinted skin tissue. http://ir.organovo.com/news/press-releases/press-releases-details/2015/LOreal-USA-Announces-Research-Partnership-with-Organovo-to-Develop-3-D--Bioprinted-Skin-Tissue/
35. Natura: Environmental commitments. https://www.naturabrasil.fr/en/our-values/environmental-commitments
36. Administration U.S. Food and Drug: Federal food, drug, and cosmetic act, USA (2010).
37. Mint: Beauty or bust. Obsessed with cosmetics. https://www.mint.com/blog/consumer-iq/splurge-vs-save-which-beauty-products-are-worth-the-extra-cost-0413/?display=wide
38. Statista.com: Revenue of the cosmetic industry in the United States from 2002 to 2016 (in billion U.S. dollars). http://www.statista.com/statistics/243742/revenue-of-the-cosmetic-industry-in-the-us/
39. AOL: Ideal to real. Body image survey. http://www.aol.com/article/2014/02/24/loveyourselfie/20836450/
40. Clynes, M.E.: Cyborgs and space. Astronautics **26**, 74–75 (1960)
41. Freedman, T., Lindner, G.: Must tomorrow's man look like this? (1963)
42. Kurzweil, R.: The Singularity is Near: When Humans Transcend Biology. Penguin, New York (2005)
43. Guga, J.: From science fiction to social reality. Beyond AI Artif. Dreams. 98 (2011)
44. Caidin, M.: Six Million Dollar Man (1974)
45. Harbisson, N., Ribas, M.: Cyborg foundation. http://www.cyborgfoundation.com
46. Google: Project jacquard. https://www.google.com/atap/project-jacquard/
47. Ringly: Ringly. https://ringly.com/
48. Lauren, R.: Polo tech shirt—RalphLauren.com. http://www.ralphlauren.com/shop/index.jsp?categoryId=46285296
49. Moon Ribas: Neil Harbisson—The world's first official cyborg. https://commons.wikimedia.org/wiki/File:Neil_Harbisson_-_The_World's_First_Official_Cyborg.jpg
50. Weiser, M.: The computer for the 21st century. Sci. Am. **265**, 94–104 (1991)
51. Sorabji, R.: Aristotle on demarcating the five senses. Philos. Rev. **80**, 55–79 (1971)
52. Kant, I., Guyer, P., Wood, A.W.: Critique of Pure Reason. Cambridge University Press, Cambridge (1999)

53. Mumford, M.D., Costanza, D.P., Connelly, M.S., Johnson, J.F.: Item generation procedures and background data scales: implications for construct and criterion-related validity. Pers. Psychol. **49**, 361–398 (1996)
54. Saponas, T.S., Tan, D.S., Morris, D., Balakrishnan, R., Turner, J., Landay, J.A.: Enabling always-available input with muscle-computer interfaces. In: Proceedings of the 22nd Annual ACM Symposium on User Interface Software and Technology, pp. 167–176 (2009)
55. Singla, R., Chambayil, B., Khosla, A., Santosh, J.: Comparison of SVM and ANN for classification of eye events in EEG. J. Biomed. Sci. Eng. **4**, 62 (2011)
56. Lai, X., Liu, Q., Wei, X., Wang, W., Zhou, G., Han, G.: A survey of body sensor networks. Sensors **13**, 5406–5447 (2013)
57. Kim, J., Mastnik, S., André, E.: EMG-based hand gesture recognition for realtime biosignal interfacing. In: Proceedings of the 13th International Conference on Intelligent User Interfaces, pp. 30–39 (2008)
58. Ugulino, W., Cardador, D., Vega, K., Velloso, E., Milidiú, R., Fuks, H.: Wearable computing: accelerometers' data classification of body postures and movements. In: Advances in Artificial Intelligence-SBIA 2012, pp. 52–61. Springer, Heidelberg (2012)
59. Wilson, A.D.: PlayAnywhere: a compact interactive tabletop projection-vision system. In: Proceedings of the 18th Annual ACM Symposium on User Interface Software and Technology, pp. 83–92 (2005)
60. Saponas, T.S., Tan, D.S., Morris, D., Turner, J., Landay, J.A.: Making muscle-computer interfaces more practical. In: Proceedings of the SIGCHI Conference on Human Factors in Computing Systems, pp. 851–854 (2010)
61. Lai, K., Konrad, J., Ishwar, P.: A gesture-driven computer interface using Kinect. In: 2012 IEEE Southwest Symposium on Image Analysis and Interpretation (SSIAI), pp. 185–188 (2012)
62. Mistry, P., Maes, P.: SixthSense: a wearable gestural interface. In: ACM SIGGRAPH ASIA 2009 Sketches, p. 11 (2009)
63. Harrison, C., Ramamurthy, S., Hudson, S.E.: On-body interaction: armed and dangerous. In: Proceedings of the Sixth International Conference on Tangible, Embedded and Embodied Interaction, pp. 69–76 (2012)
64. Abawajy, J.H.: Human-computer interaction in ubiquitous computing environments. Int. J. Pervasive Comput. Commun. **5**, 61–77 (2009)
65. Kapur, A., Kapur, A., Virji-Babul, N., Tzanetakis, G., Driessen, P.F.: Gesture-based affective computing on motion capture data. In: Proceedings of the 1st International Conference on Affective Computing and Intelligent Interaction, pp. 1–7. Springer (2005)
66. Gunes, H., Piccardi, M.: Automatic visual recognition of face and body action units. In: Third International Conference on Information Technology and Applications, 2005. ICITA 2005, pp. 668–673 (2005)
67. Van Duinen, H., Gandevia, S.C.: Constraints for control of the human hand. J. Physiol. **589**, 5583–5593 (2011)
68. Pentland, A.P.: Wearable Intelligence. Scientific American, Incorporated (1998)
69. Jablonski, N.G.: Skin: A Natural History. University of California Press, Berkeley (2013)
70. Pearson, I.: Active skin. https://timeguide.wordpress.com
71. L'Oreal: Makeup genius. http://www.lorealparisusa.com/en/brands/makeup/makeup-genius-virtual-makeup-tool.aspx
72. SunFriend: UVA+B Sunfriend. http://sunfriend.com/
73. Mink: Mink x makers. http://hellomink.com/shop/makeup-printer
74. William, P., Steven, K., Sharma, S.: Wanderers: wearables for interplanetary pilgrims. http://matter.media.mit.edu/environments/details/wanderers-wearables-for-interplanetary-pilgrims
75. Vega, K., Fuks, H.: Beauty technology: body surface computing. Comput. (Long. Beach. Calif) **47**, 71–75 (2014)
76. Vega, K., Fuks, H.: Beauty tech nails: interactive technology at your fingertips. In: Proceedings of the 8th International Conference on Tangible, Embedded and Embodied Interaction, pp. 61–64 (2014)

77. Takara Tomy Arts: Lumi deco nail stickers. http://shop.whiterabbitjapan.com/products/lumi-deco-nail-stickers
78. Vega, K., Arrieta, A., Esteves, F., Fuks, H.: FX e-makeup for muscle based interaction. In: Design, User Experience, and Usability. User Experience Design for Everyday Life Applications and Services, pp. 643–652. Springer International Publishing (2014)
79. Weigel, M., Lu, T., Bailly, G., Oulasvirta, A., Majidi, C., Steimle, J.: iSkin: flexible, stretchable and visually customizable on-body touch sensors for mobile computing. In: Proceedings of the 33rd Annual ACM Conference on Human Factors in Computing Systems, pp. 2991–3000. ACM, New York (2015)
80. Tribe, J., Whittow, W., Batchelor, J.: Aesthetically enhanced RFID inkjet antenna logos on skin (AERIALS). In: Design, User Experience, and Usability. User Experience Design for Everyday Life Applications and Services, pp. 719–730. Springer (2014)
81. Mistry, P., Ishii, K., Inami, M., Igarashi, T.: Blinkbot: look at, blink and move. In: Adjunct Proceedings of the 23nd Annual ACM Symposium on User Interface Software and Technology, pp. 397–398 (2010)
82. Salvucci, D.D., Anderson, J.R.: Automated eye-movement protocol analysis. Hum. Comput. Interact. **16**, 39–86 (2001)
83. Bulling, A., Roggen, D., Tröster, G.: It's in your eyes: towards context-awareness and mobile HCI using wearable EOG goggles. Proceedings of the 10th international conference on Ubiquitous computing. pp. 84–93 (2008).
84. Horng, W.-B., Chen, C.-Y., Chang, Y., Fan, C.-H.: Driver fatigue detection based on eye tracking and dynamk, template matching. In: 2004 IEEE International Conference on Networking, Sensing and Control, pp. 7–12 (2004)
85. Królak, A., Strumillo, P.: Fatigue monitoring by means of eye blink analysis in image sequences. ICSES **1**, 219–222 (2006)
86. Zhou, Z.-H., Geng, X.: Projection functions for eye detection. Pattern Recogn. **37**, 1049–1056 (2004)
87. Królak, A., Strumillo, P.: Eye-blink detection system for human—computer interaction. Univ. Access Inf. Soc. **11**, 409–419 (2012)
88. Grauman, K., Betke, M., Lombardi, J., Gips, J., Bradski, G.R.: Communication via eye blinks and eyebrow raises: video-based human-computer interfaces. Univ. Access Inf. Soc. **2**, 359–373 (2003)
89. Park, K.S., Lee, K.T.: Eye-controlled human/computer interface using the line-of-sight and the intentional blink. Comput. Ind. Eng. **30**, 463–473 (1996)
90. Miles, W.R.: Elevation of the eye-balls on winking. J. Exp. Psychol. **14**, 311 (1931)
91. Sydney VIVID Festival: Haptic Interface Pop Up (2013)
92. Asian Premiere of Multimedia Art: New York Paris Hong Kong Change your Perception: Blinklifier (2013)
93. Wearable, B.: Blinklifier (2012)
94. Haptic Interface Exhibition: Blinklifier. http://hapticinterface.hkbu.edu.hk/?page_id=30
95. Vega, K.: Conversatorio Fundación Telefónica: Arte y Estética en Wearable Computers. Arcana, Gimmickiano, AquaDJing (2013)
96. Vega, K.: Superhero—Design Challenge TEI'13. http://www.tei-conf.org/13/dc
97. Bare Conductive: Conductive Ink. http://www.bareconductive.com/
98. Vega, K., Aucelio, R., Fuks, H.: Hairware: designing conductive hair extensions for seamless interfaces. In: Design, User Experience, and Usability: Users and Interactions, pp. 696–704. Springer (2015)
99. Vega, K., Cunha, M., Fuks, H.: Hairware: the conscious use of unconscious auto-contact behaviors. In: Proceedings of the 20th International Conference on Intelligent User Interfaces, pp. 78–86. ACM, New York, (2015)
100. Vega, K., Cunha, M., Fuks, H.: Hairware: conductive hair extensions as a capacitive touch input device. In: Proceedings of the 20th International Conference on Intelligent User Interfaces Companion, pp. 89–92. ACM, New York (2015)

101. Lee, H.M., Choi, S.-Y., Jung, A., Ko, S.H.: Highly conductive aluminum textile and paper for flexible and wearable electronics. Angew. Chemie. **125**, 7872–7877 (2013)
102. Locher, I., Kirstein, T., Tröster, G.: Routing methods adapted to e-textiles. In: Proceedings of 37th International Symposium on Microelectronics (IMAPS). Long Beach (2004)
103. Vega, K., Fuks, H.: Empowering electronic divas through beauty technology. Lecture Notes in Computer Science, pp. 237–245. Springer (2013)
104. Vega, K., Fuks, H.: Beauty technology as an interactive computing platform. In: Proceedings of the 2013 ACM International Conference on Interactive Tabletops and Surfaces, pp. 357–360. ACM, New York (2013)
105. Tobita, H., Kuzi, T.: SmartWig: wig-based wearable computing device for communication and entertainment. In: Proceedings of the International Working Conference on Advanced Visual Interfaces, pp. 299–302 (2012)
106. Sign, F.: Products—First sign. http://www.firstsign.us/products/
107. Hallpike, C.R.: Social hair. Man **4**, 256–264 (1969)
108. Webster, J.G.: Medical instrumentation Application and Design. Houghton Mifflin, Boston 197& g. (1973)
109. Streitz, N., Kameas, A., Mavrommati, I.: The Disappearing Computer: Interaction Design, System Infrastructures and Applications for Smart Environments. Springer, Berlin (2007)
110. Norman, D.A.: The Invisible Computer: Why Good Products can Fail, the Personal Computer is so Complex, and Information Appliances are the Solution. MIT Press, Cambridge (1998)
111. O2: Talk to the hand—O$_2$ upcycle. http://news.o2.co.uk/?press-release=talk-to-the-hand-o2-upcycle#
112. Mistry, P.: SixthSense. http://www.pranavmistry.com/projects/sixthsense/
113. Saponas, T.S., Harrison, C., Benko, H.: PocketTouch: through-fabric capacitive touch input. In: Proceedings of the 24th Annual ACM Symposium on User Interface Software and Technology, pp. 303–308 (2011)
114. Charlesworth, J.: Wearables as "relationship tools". AI Soc. **22**, 63–84 (2007)
115. Schwarz, J., Harrison, C., Hudson, S., Mankoff, J.: Cord input: an intuitive, high-accuracy, multi-degree-of-freedom input method for mobile devices. In: Proceedings of the SIGCHI Conference on Human Factors in Computing Systems, pp. 1657–1660 (2010)
116. Duncan Jr., S.: Nonverbal communication. Psychol. Bull. **72**, 118 (1969)
117. Ekman, P., Friesen, W. V: The repertoire of nonverbal behavior: categories, origins, usage, and coding. In: Nonverbal Communication, Interaction, and Gesture, pp. 57–106. Mouton, The Hague (1981)
118. Morris, D., Desebrock, G.: Manwatching: A Field Guide to Human Behaviour. HN Abrams, New York (1977)
119. Vega, K.: Hairware video. https://youtu.be/VAmpGjVCSbI
120. Web4camguy: Grace #40 of 100 Strangers. https://www.flickr.com/photos/web4camguy/7177165966
121. Erin, E.: Aaaarrrggghhh. https://www.flickr.com/photos/evilerin/3078856253/in/photostream/
122. Pilbrow, S.: Hair pulling stress. https://www.flickr.com/photos/stuartpilbrow/3345896050
123. BigML: BigML. https://bigml.com/
124. Windmiller, J.R., Wang, J.: Wearable electrochemical sensors and biosensors: a review. Electroanalysis **25**, 29–46 (2013)
125. Tharion, W.J., Buller, M.J., Karis, A.J., Mullen, S.P.: Acceptability of a wearable vital sign detection system. In: Proceedings of the Human Factors and Ergonomics Society Annual Meeting, pp. 1006–1010 (2007)
126. Bitarello, B., Fuks, H., Queiroz, J.: New technologies for dynamic tattoo art. In: Proceedings of the Fifth International Conference on Tangible, Embedded, and Embodied Interaction, pp. 313–316 (2011)
127. mc10: MC10 reshaping electronics. http://www.mc10inc.com/company-information/technology/
128. Rotter, P., Daskala, B., Compano, R.: RFID implants: opportunities and challenges for identifying people. IEEE Technol. Soc. Mag. **27**, 24–32 (2008)

129. Foster, K.R., Jaeger, J.: RFID inside. IEEE Spectr. **44**, 24–29 (2007)
130. Ding, L.: Digitize eyeshadow. http://dlulin.com/projects/digital-eyeshadow/
131. Lin, M., Li, B.: A wireless EOG-based human computer interface. In: 2010 3rd International Conference on Biomedical Engineering and Informatics (BMEI), pp. 1794–1796 (2010)
132. Curran, E., Sykacek, P., Stokes, M., Roberts, S.J., Penny, W., Johnsrude, I., Owen, A.M.: Cognitive tasks for driving a brain-computer interfacing system: a pilot study. IEEE Trans. Neural Syst. Rehabil. Eng. **12**, 48–54 (2004)
133. Tanaka, K., Matsunaga, K., Hori, S.: Electroencephalogram-based control of a mobile robot. Electr. Eng. Jpn. **152**, 39–46 (2005)
134. Fabiani, G.E., McFarland, D.J., Wolpaw, J.R., Pfurtscheller, G.: Conversion of EEG activity into cursor movement by a brain-computer interface (BCI). IEEE Trans. Neural Syst. Rehabil. Eng. **12**, 331–338 (2004)
135. Kanade, T., Cohn, J.F., Tian, Y.: Comprehensive database for facial expression analysis. In: Proceedings of the Fourth IEEE International Conference on Automatic Face and Gesture Recognition, 2000, pp. 46–53 (2000)
136. Izard, C.E.: The Maximally Discriminitive Facial Movements Coding System, MAX. University of Delaware, Newark (1979)
137. Ekman, P.: Facial expression and emotion. Am. Psychol. **48**, 384 (1993)
138. Scherer, K.R., Ekman, P.: Handbook of Methods in Nonverbal Behavior Research. University Press Cambridge, Cambridge (1982)
139. Ekman, P., Friesen, W.V.: Measuring facial movement. Environ. Psychol. Nonverbal Behav. **1**, 56–75 (1976)
140. Tsakiris, M.: On agency and body-ownership. In: Experience Subjective Pre Reflexive & Action (ESPRA) Conference, CREA, Paris (2005)
141. Rantanen, V., Venesvirta, H., Spakov, O., Verho, J., Vetek, A., Surakka, V., Lekkala, J.: Capacitive measurement of facial activity intensity. IEEE Sensors J. **13**, 4329–4338 (2013)
142. Manabe, D.: Face visualizer, face instrument. http://www.daito.ws/
143. Saponas, T.S., Kelly, D., Parviz, B.A., Tan, D.S.: Optically sensing tongue gestures for computer input. In: Proceedings of the 22nd Annual ACM Symposium on User Interface Software and Technology, pp. 177–180 (2009)
144. Gallagher, S.: Self reference and schizophrenia. Explor. self. 203–239 (2000)
145. Tsakiris, M., Schuetz-Bosbach, S., Gallagher, S.: On agency and body-ownership: phenomenological and neurocognitive reflections. Conscious. Cogn. **16**, 645–660 (2007)
146. Tsakiris, M., Prabhu, G., Haggard, P.: Having a body versus moving your body: how agency structures body-ownership. Conscious. Cogn. **15**, 423–432 (2006)
147. Rinn, W.E.: The neuropsychology of facial expression: a review of the neurological and psychological mechanisms for producing facial expressions. Psychol. Bull. **95**, 52 (1984)
148. De Boulogne, G.-B.D., Cuthbertson, R.A.: The Mechanism of Human Facial Expression. Cambridge University Press, Cambridge (1990)
149. Ekman, P., Roper, G., Hager, J.C.: Deliberate facial movement. Child Dev. **51**, 886–891 (1980)
150. Gosselin, P., Perron, M., Beaupré, M.: The voluntary control of facial action units in adults. Emotion **10**, 266 (2010)
151. Vega, K.: KINISI video. https://www.youtube.com/watch?v=7JrRo1U7c5o
152. Lathem, P.A., Gregorio, T.L., Garber, S.L.: High-level quadriplegia: an occupational therapy challenge. Am. J. Occup. Ther. **39**, 705–714 (1985)
153. Sipski, M.L., Richards, J.S.: Spinal cord injury rehabilitation: state of the science. Am. J. Phys. Med. Rehabil. **85**, 310–342 (2006)
154. Wimmer, R., Echtler, F.: Exploring the benefits of fingernail displays. In: CHI'13 Extended Abstracts on Human Factors in Computing Systems, pp. 937–942 (2013)
155. Su, C.-H., Chan, L., Weng, C.-T., Liang, R.-H., Cheng, K.-Y., Chen, B.-Y.: NailDisplay: bringing an always available visual display to fingertips. In: Proceedings of the SIGCHI Conference on Human Factors in Computing Systems, pp. 1461–1464 (2013)

156. Weigel, M., Steimle, J.: Fingernail displays: handy displays at your fingertips. In: CHI'13 Extended Abstracts on Human Factors in Computing Systems, pp. 937–942 (2013)

157. Fukumoto, M., Suenaga, Y.: "FingeRing": a full-time wearable interface. In: Conference Companion on Human Factors in Computing Systems, pp. 81–82 (1994)

158. Ketabdar, H., Moghadam, P., Roshandel, M.: Pingu: a new miniature wearable device for ubiquitous computing environments. In: 2012 Sixth International Conference on Complex, Intelligent and Software Intensive Systems (CISIS), pp. 502–506 (2012)

159. Ashbrook, D., Baudisch, P., White, S.: Nenya: subtle and eyes-free mobile input with a magnetically-tracked finger ring. In: Proceedings of the SIGCHI Conference on Human Factors in Computing Systems, pp. 2043–2046 (2011)

160. Harrison, C., Hudson, S.E.: Abracadabra: wireless, high-precision, and unpowered finger input for very small mobile devices. In: Proceedings of the 22nd Annual ACM Symposium on User Interface Software and Technology, pp. 121–124 (2009)

161. Hinckley, K., Wigdor, D.: Input technologies and techniques. In: The Human-Computer Interaction Handbook: Fundamentals, Evolving Technologies, and Emerging Applications, pp. 151–168 (2002)

162. Lepinski, G.J., Grossman, T., Fitzmaurice, G.: The design and evaluation of multitouch marking menus. In: Proceedings of the SIGCHI Conference on Human Factors in Computing Systems, pp. 2233–2242 (2010)

163. Dietz, P., Leigh, D.: DiamondTouch: a multi-user touch technology. In: Proceedings of the 14th Annual ACM Symposium on User Interface Software and Technology, pp. 219–226 (2001)

164. Willingham, D.B.: A neuropsychological theory of motor skill learning. Psychol. Rev. **105**, 558 (1998)

165. Card, S.K., Mackinlay, J.D., Robertson, G.G.: A morphological analysis of the design space of input devices. ACM Trans. Inf. Syst. **9**, 99–122 (1991)

166. Rekimoto, J.: Gesturewrist and gesturepad: unobtrusive wearable interaction devices. In: Proceedings of the Fifth International Symposium on Wearable Computers, 2001, pp. 21–27 (2001)

167. Roberts, C.M.: Radio frequency identification (RFID). Comput. Secur. **25**, 18–26 (2006)

168. Innovations, I.: Innovated RFID product. http://www.id-innovations.com/httpdocs/ Modules(non write).htm

169. Want, R.: An introduction to RFID technology. IEEE Pervasive Comput. **5**, 25–33 (2006)

170. Research, B.: Wearable technology application chart. http://www.beechamresearch.com/ article.aspx?id=20

171. Vega, K.F.C., Flanagan, P.J., Fuks, H.: Blinklifier: a case study for prototyping wearable computers in technology and visual arts. In: Design, User Experience, and Usability. User Experience in Novel Technological Environments, pp. 439–445. Springer, Heidelberg (2013)

172. XO, S.: e-Pannosa. https://www.youtube.com/watch?v=ahohyw2CJgs

173. Kao, H.-L. (Cindy), Dementyev, A., Paradiso, J.A., Schmandt, C.: NailO: fingernails as an input surface. In: Proceedings of the 33rd Annual ACM Conference on Human Factors in Computing Systems, pp. 3015–3018. ACM, New York (2015)

174. Lochner, C.M., Khan, Y., Pierre, A., Arias, A.C.: All-organic optoelectronic sensor for pulse oximetry. Nat. Commun. **5**, 5745 (2014)

175. Google: Introducing our smart contact lens. http://googleblog.blogspot.com/2014/01/intro-ducing-our-smart-contact-lens.html

Index

A
AquaDjing, 63–68, 70, 72
Arcana circuit, 24
Auto-contact behavior, 29, 33, 34, 38, 41

B
Beauty Tech Nails
    AquaDJing, 63
    human factors, 58
    non-contact interaction, 61
    RFID based interaction, 59–60
    RFID tags, 59
    RFIDs' dimensions, 60
Beauty technology
    bio data, 10
    computational vision, 10
    context of application, 12
    facial expressions, 11
    finger movements, 12
    Human Computer Interaction studies, 11
    interactive cosmetics, 15
    Micro Movements, 11
    multilayer classification, 14
    taxonomy, 11
Beauty technology book organization, 7
Beltility, 61–64
Black fake eyelashes, 21
Black metalized fake eyelashes, 22
Blinking interaction, 19–20
Blinklifier project, 21, 25
Blombos Cave, 3

C
Capacitor sensor, 37
Communication sector, 72, 73
Concealed interaction, 32, 33
Conductive eyelashes
    BlinkBot, 18
    control and command, 18
Conductive Makeup, 25
Conductive makeup design, 20
Cosmetics
    cultural and religious aspects, 3
    customers, 4
    global beauty business market, 4
    oils and creams, 3
Cyborg fashion, 4, 5

D
DiamondTouch, 58
Do-It-Yourself (DIY) gateway, 2

E
Electroencephalogram (EEG), 10
Electromyogram (EMG), 10
Electronic Divas, 21
Electrooculography (EOG), 10, 18

F
Facial Action Code System (FACS), 46
FX e-makeup

© Springer International Publishing Switzerland 2016
K. Vega, H. Fuks, *Beauty Technology*, Human–Computer Interaction Series,
DOI 10.1007/978-3-319-15762-7

FX e-makeup (*cont.*)
    bio-potential sensors, 44
    design, 45, 46
    eyebrow sensor, 49
    facial actions, 44–45
    sensors, 48

G
Glamor sector, 70, 72

H
Hairware
    chemical process, 29–30
    electrochemical process, 30
    features, 30
    geotemporal factors, 38
    input device, 31–40
    interfaces, 27, 28
    natural coloration, 27
    non-conductive artificial hair extension, 38
    output device, 30–31
    security device, 39
Hardware, 34
Human–computer interaction, 32

K
Kinisi, 46, 48, 50, 51, 70

L
LED eyelashes, 3, 7
Lifestyle computing sector, 72, 73
Lumi Deco Nails, 70

M
Makeup Genius (L'Oreal), 13
Medical sector, 73, 74

N
Nail interfaces
    finger muscles, 58

    finger-worn devices, 58
    OLED display, 58

P
Pearson's vision, 12

S
Security and safety sector, 74, 75
Sensing blinking, 18
Skin interfaces
    electronic devices, 44
    Mc10, 44
Smile sensor, 49
Software, 35, 38
Sport and fitness sector, 73, 74
Superhero blinks, 26

T
Tech nails to wearables, 61
TEI 2013 Design Challenge, 22
Temporary Transfer Tattoo, 44
Twinkle nails, 61, 62, 68, 70, 72

U
U.S. Food and Drug Administration, 14

W
Wearable computing
    cognitive technology, 1
    electronic skins, 2
    human body characteristics, 2
    Lilypad Arduino, 1
    materials, 2
Wearables
    clothes and accessories, 69
    communication and glamor, 70
    human body, 69
    Invisible Computing Paradigm, 69
    revolution, 2
Wellness sector, 73, 74
Winkymote, 46, 51–55, 74

Printed in the United States
By Bookmasters